WHEN OUTLAWS WORE BADGES

MELODY GROVES

TWODOT®

GUILFORD, CONNECTICUT
HELENA, MONTANA

A · T W O D O T® · B O O K
An imprint of The Rowman & Littlefield Publishing Group, Inc.
4501 Forbes Blvd., Ste. 200
Lanham, MD 20706
www.rowman.com

Distributed by NATIONAL BOOK NETWORK

British Library Cataloguing in Publication Information available

Library of Congress Control Number: 2020950357

ISBN 978-1-4930-4803-8 (paper : alk. paper)
ISBN 978-1-4930-4804-5 (electronic)

∞™ The paper used in this publication meets the minimum requirements of American National Standard for Information Sciences—Permanence of Paper for Printed Library Materials, ANSI/NISO Z39.48-1992.

CONTENTS

Contents

Acknowledgments

A voluminous thank you to:

Myke Groves, photography acquisition assistant

Marc Ferguson, curator at Dalton's Hideout, Meade, Kansas

Rough Riders Museum, Las Vegas, New Mexico

Judy Avila, Joyce Hertzog, Phil Jackson, Dennis Kastendiek, Kathy Wagoner, Bill Pinnell, editorial assistants

INTRODUCTION

TWO MEN . . . BOTH HEELED . . . STAND IN THE MIDDLE OF THE street . . . legs apart . . . eyes squinting into steely stares. Hands hover over the butts of their holstered revolvers. . . . And then . . . a twitch . . . an eye tic . . . like lightning, hands slap leather. Hammers pull back. Point.

Bang!

Bang!

One walks away.

Lawman or outlaw? Black-hatted villains and white-hatted good guys of the Old West walked the streets of our imagination. Hollywood drew a convenient line in the Western dirt, differentiating between the two. But in reality, at times it was difficult, if not impossible, to distinguish who was who. Shadowy faces roamed the West.

In his biography *Wyatt Earp: The Life behind the Legend* (1997), Casey Tefertiller writes that Earp "became a vigilante, a marshal, and an outlaw all at the same time." Convinced that law no longer protected law-abiding citizens in Tombstone, Arizona Territory, Earp moved outside legal boundaries to bring what he considered order and justice to a chaotic situation.

His dilemma was nothing new in the West. Mid- to late nineteenth-century frontier areas, including mining camps such as Deadwood, found themselves reinventing laws and society. Cow towns such as Wichita, Abilene, and Dodge City faced a constant barrage of change, resulting in instability. Even small commercial towns such as Lincoln, New Mexico Territory, exemplified these chaotic times. So, is it any wonder the lines between lawman and outlaw were blurred?

Westerners blazed away at each other with Colt revolvers, Winchester carbines, and double-barrel shotguns. Gunfighters . . . shootists . . . pistoleros . . . leather slappers . . . gunmen . . . buscaderos—men of the West exposed themselves to peril by wearing badges, robbing people, or associating with dangerous men in dangerous places. Sometimes, they did it all at once. And which side of the badge the gunfighters were on made it legal or not.

Unlike Old West movies, where the outlaw was always a grizzled, mean, and murdering road agent and the lawman was a calm, steely-eyed, honest man, the reality was that the two types were very much alike. Some were known to have been good men, such as Bat Masterson, Heck Thomas, and Bill Tilghman. But even a young Bill Tilghman was once charged with stealing, and so was Wyatt Earp.

What the lawmen and outlaws had in common, besides their gun handling, was the willingness to risk their lives to enforce the law or to commit a crime. There were various types of lawmen in the Old West. There were US marshals, selected by the attorney general; sheriffs elected to office by county residents; marshals chosen by the city council; and deputies, constables, rangers, and peace officers.

Many lawmen received no pay other than a percentage of any money that those they arrested might be fined, or the collection of bounties on the heads of wanted men. This often led them to have second jobs, or to sometimes use their badges in establishing protection rackets or other crimes. Pay was often very low for those who did make a salary, and their duties included tasks that many felt were beneath them, such as keeping the street clean, or in the case of US marshals, being responsible for taking the federal census and distributing presidential proclamations. Often their work consisted of boring tasks punctuated by moments of high drama and accentuated by deadly confrontation.

CHAPTER ONE

Milton J. Yarberry: Albuquerque's First Town Marshal, "Jerked to Jesus"

Young man, lay away your gun. Remember poor Yarberry.
—Santa Fe Daily New Mexican, February 10, 1883

Hollywood couldn't write an Old West character better than Milton J. Yarberry, Albuquerque's first town marshal. Trigger-happy Yarberry met his demise at the end of a hangman's noose, when, on February 9, 1883, he uttered his final words, "Gentlemen, you are hanging an innocent man," before being "jerked to Jesus."

He Started Young

Yarberry, who started life probably as John Armstrong in Walnut Ridge, Arkansas, in 1849, turned to crime at an early age. Using several aliases over his lifetime, as a young teenager, he began his criminal career by killing a man over a land dispute. On the run, he changed his name for the first time, claiming he could not bring shame to his family. In 1873, he killed a man in Helena, Sharp County, Arkansas, and again fled.

According to all contemporary reports, Yarberry was not a handsome man. Long, lanky, and slightly stooped, he stood six

Albuquerque's first Town Marshal was hanged in 1883.
AUTHOR'S COLLECTION

foot three without boots and walked with a peculiar, loose-jointed, shambling gait. A "long, crane-like neck" supported his "small, poorly-developed head," with its dark hair and mustache, restless cold grey eyes, straight thin nose, and mouth "expressing chiefly cunning and cruelty." One reporter, after interviewing him, concluded he lacked the mentality to distinguish between a legal and an illegal act.

RUSTLING

During the 1870s, Yarberry rode with outlaws Dave Rudabaugh and "Mysterious Dave" Mather (who also associated with Billy the Kid) and beginning in 1873, operated mostly in southern Missouri and northern Arkansas. The three formed a cattle-rustling outfit, engaged in several robberies, and were implicated in the murder of a well-known rancher in Arkansas.

Yarberry and the boys hightailed it to Texas and scattered. For a time, Yarberry settled in Texarkana, the "rendezvous of more criminals than any spot in the West," but moved when he met a man he suspected of being a bounty hunter. Understandably nervous, Yarberry, convinced someone was trailing him, always looking over his shoulder, thought a man walking behind him was a detective. He shot and killed him. It turned out the victim was an "inoffensive traveler."

Yarberry's bounty for the Sharp County murder was two hundred dollars.

NOW A TEXAS RANGER? SERIOUSLY?

In Texas, it looked like he'd turned his life around. Still on the dodge, he served in the Texas Rangers' Company B of the Frontier Battalion, stationed in Jack County, Texas. According to sketchy records, Yarberry served honorably, but only for a short time—about a month or so. Relocating to Decatur, Texas, calling himself John Johnson, he opened a saloon and billiard parlor. Once again, a bounty hunter stopped by asking about Yarberry in relation to the Sharp County murder. Within hours, Yarberry sold out to his partner and left town. Days later, the bounty hunter's body was found near Decatur, riddled with bullet holes.

ON BECOMING A BROTHEL OWNER

From Decatur, Yarberry rode to Dodge City, Kansas, where he spent a brief time, and then by early 1878 he had opened a saloon-brothel-variety theater in Canon City, Colorado.

Nineteenth-century entertainer Eddie Foy played there and in his memoirs, according to Robert K. DeArment in his *Deadly Dozen: Twelve Forgotten Gunfighters of the Old West*, stated that Yarberry "fashioned himself a good violinist." Foy described his employer as "citified" and "prosperous-appearing" in a "broadcloth suit, velvet vest, frilled shirt front and white collar . . . expensive Eastern-made boots, and a long, black mustache, [but] none too sweet a character."

Yarberry was slow to pay his suppliers and performers. After several weeks of entertaining, Foy and his partner finished and asked for pay. They were not able to collect it all. For partial payment, Foy's partner stole a barrel of whiskey and sold it. DeArment reports that Foy wrote that he was surprised at his partner's courage "in daring to pull such a trick on a man of this type . . . he was not the sort that would hesitate to take direct and violent action when it suited his mood to do so."

In March 1879, a bartender of a rival saloon shot Yarberry's partner Tony Preston, wounding him seriously but not killing him. Yarberry shot at the man, missed, then joined the posse in pursuit. He returned to Canon City, sold out to Preston, and headed out of town.

Yarberry joined the hell-on-wheels crowd following the construction gangs of the Santa Fe Railroad, who were building south through New Mexico. With a female Mexican partner remembered only as "Steamboat," he operated brothels in a succession of railroad boom camps.

Settling in Las Vegas, New Mexico Territory, he opened a brothel catering to the railroad workers. Suspected of robbing and murdering a freighter during this time, he was never charged. In 1879, still known as a member of the Dodge City Gang, he shot and killed a man in the Rincon Hotel, allegedly over a prostitute.

With associates in the Dodge City Gang such as Hyman G. Neill (aka "Hoodoo Brown"), Tom Pickett, Joe Carson, "Big Jim"

Dunagain, Bill Goodlet, John Henry "Doc" Holliday, and others, there is little doubt about how Milton J. Yarberry earned a living. Selling his share of the brothel, he moved to San Marcial, New Mexico, where his former partner Tony Preston had settled, still recovering from being shot. After he arrived, Yarberry continued the affair he'd previously had with Preston's wife Sadie. When Yarberry left San Marcial, he took Sadie and her four-year-old daughter with him. They relocated to the brand-new town of Albuquerque, New Mexico, in 1880.

BECOMING THE LAW IN ALBUQUERQUE

Albuquerque, with its just-completed railroad, boomed with new people and spiraling crime. Somehow befriending Sheriff Perfecto Armijo of Bernalillo County, New Mexico, Yarberry was appointed Albuquerque's first town marshal—a lawman paid by merchants. Illiterate, he was a drunken loudmouth and a bully, a poor fit for the job. Yarberry proved this by killing two men a short time later. In 1881, Harry Brown, a member of a prominent Tennessee family (his father and uncle had both served as governor), claimed to be a gunman and drifted into town, gaining a reputation as a heavy drinker with a temper and a habit of pulling his gun with little provocation.

Sadie's romantic attentions turned to Brown, and Yarberry was unaware. By happenstance, in March 1881, Yarberry discovered them downtown at Gerard's Restaurant. The two men walked to a nearby vacant lot and continued arguing, during which time Brown repeatedly told Yarberry he was not afraid of him. Sadie Preston then appeared in the doorway of the restaurant and called for Brown. Brown immediately hit Yarberry in the face, while at the same time Brown drew his pistol. Brown fired once, creasing Yarberry in the hand, at which point Yarberry drew his own pistol and took two shots at Brown, in quick succession, hitting him in the chest. Brown died immediately.

Downtown Albuquerque circa 1881.
PHOTO BY COBB STUDIO, COURTESY ALBUQUERQUE MUSEUM

YARBERRY ACQUITTED OF MURDER

Three months later, the town marshal, known to be a drinker, sat on a friend's front porch when he heard gunshots. Yarberry ran to where a bystander pointed to a man walking down the street. He called out to stop, but the man continued. Yarberry fired numerous times, killing him. It turned out the victim was an unarmed railroad carpenter who did not even own a gun. The lawman was cleared in a preliminary hearing, leading to a loud public outcry, despite evidence at the time that Yarberry acted in good faith and out of self-defense. However, the self-defense plea didn't work in the next hearing.

In 1882, a grand jury indicted Yarberry for the carpenter's murder. Timing, as they say, is everything. And for Yarberry, it was bad timing. New Mexico's new governor, Lionel Sheldon, chose to be tough and make an example out of Yarberry since news stories of Billy the Kid were running rampant. The Santa Fe trial lasted three days, after which Yarberry was convicted, sentenced to hang. All appeals were overturned. After the disappointing news, Yarberry was told that he looked pale, and he replied, "Maybe. But I ain't sick, and I ain't scared either."

On February 9, 1883, under a guard of New Mexico militia made up of the Governor's Rifles, Yarberry was marched to the gallows at the Albuquerque courthouse. His close friend, Sheriff Perfecto Armijo, was tasked with pulling the lever to hang him. Over 1,500 people watched, many paying a dollar for the privilege. As Sheriff Armijo pulled the lever, Yarberry proclaimed, "Gentlemen, you are hanging an innocent man."

JERKED TO JESUS

Yarberry was hanged by means of an innovative contraption that jerked the condemned upward instead of dropping him through a trapdoor. Much controversy surrounded the marshal's death. As he jerked up, his head hit a crossbeam. Was blunt force trauma the actual cause, or was it a good "neck stretching"? Regardless, this method was never used again in New Mexico. The *Las Vegas Optic* coined the term "jerked to Jesus."

AFTERWORD

The Santa Fe paper editorialized that the hanging marked the end of the gunfighter era, which had brought such notoriety to the West and New Mexico Territory especially. "The day has passed when the illustrious braves of the west, such as Yarberry was, shall walk about in the bright sunlight, the envy and admiration of

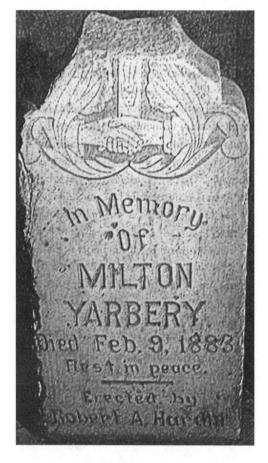

Yarberry was buried with the noose around his neck.
PHOTO BY ANDY GREGG, COURTESY ALBUQUERQUE POLICE MUSEUM

lesser lights in the criminal crowds who assemble to burn incense before them."

Milton J. Yarberry, thirty-three, was buried in Albuquerque's Santa Barbara Cemetery, with the noose still around his neck. His tombstone—with name misspelled—is now missing.

Chapter Two

Henry Plummer:
Wrongly—or Rightly—Hanged?

No man stands higher in the estimation of the community than Henry Plummer.

—Sacramento Union

Did thirty-two-year-old Henry Plummer deserve to die swinging from the proverbial cottonwood? After all, he'd killed more than a handful of men, abandoned a woman with her three little children, robbed stages, formed a gang of road agents, and even "played dead." Was he, indeed, the miscreant, the villain, the outlaw of song and lore? Maybe.

But maybe he was the man who tried to stop injustices and ended up with a noose around his neck. Maybe the Montana vigilantes, who took matters into their own hands to put an end to the robberies and murders, were wrong. They claimed Plummer was leader of "Plummer's Gang," also known as the Innocents.

"The Innocents"? Is That Ironic or What?

The question begs an answer. In 1993, some 129 years after Plummer's death, a posthumous trial (Montana's Twin Bridges Public Schools initiated the event) was held in the Virginia City,

HENRY PLUMMER

No 5.   *Philadelphia, Apr. 17 1890*   Price: 5 Cents

Henry Plummer, according to Nevada City residents, "became as bold and determined as a lion."

Montana, courthouse. The twelve registered voters on the jury were split six–six on the verdict, which led the judge to declare a mistrial. Had Plummer been alive, most likely he would have been freed and not tried again. But in reality, Plummer spent most of his years straddling the line between lawman and outlaw.

Early Years

William Henry Handy Plumer (he added the extra *m* in California) was born in 1832 in Addison, Maine, the youngest of seven children. His parents provided him and his siblings with a good, early education in a village near their farm. Considered good-looking, intelligent, and adventuresome but consumptive, he chose not to continue the family business. His father, older brother, and brother-in-law were all seafaring captains, and Plummer was expected to take to the sea. Slight of build and in fragile health, the rigors of the sea trade were too much for him to handle.

Struck with Gold Fever

In 1851, when Plummer was eighteen, his father died, leaving the family almost destitute. Struck with gold fever, Plummer promised his mother he would travel to the California gold fields and strike it rich. He headed west in April 1852, sailing out of New York to Panama, across the isthmus, then up to San Francisco. Unusual for the times, the trip took a mere twenty-four days.

California Bound

Landing in San Francisco, he immediately went to work at a bakery, saving enough money within a year to move to the mining camp of Nevada City, California (150 miles north of San Francisco). A year after landing on the West Coast, he owned a ranch and a mine outside Nevada City. Another year later, he had traded his mining shares for the Empire Bakery in Nevada City.

Henry Plummer was on his way. He sent money back home to his mother with enough left over to lead the good life. Taken with his gumption and ability to make money, by 1856 local residents asked him to run for marshal. Well liked by the citizens and respected for his promptness and boldness in handling his duties, he surprisingly won the election narrowly. At the age of twenty-four, he became marshal of Nevada City, the third-largest settlement in California. The job offered state prominence.

He handily won reelection in 1857. Then his good fortune changed. Here's where the story gets split in two. One faction reports he had an affair with the wife of a miner, John Vedder. They ended up in a duel and Plummer killed him. The other faction paints a totally different picture: John Vedder was an inept gambler who not only abused his wife Lucy, but also at times abandoned her and their sickly daughter. Desperate to find housing in the overcrowded town, Vedder turned to Henry Plummer for advice. After listening to Vedder's plea, Plummer vacated his own home and allowed the Vedders to rent it. This was his first mistake.

Within days, neighbors heard Lucy screaming in agony and discovered Vedder banging her head against the floor. Other days, they would hear her begging for mercy. On another occasion, a neighbor reported watching Vedder knock Lucy to the floor and then "pinch her nose until she could scarcely get her breath." Plummer was informed and rushed to help Lucy. This was his second mistake.

Plans were made for Lucy and the child to take the 2 a.m. stage away from the abusive husband. On the night she was to catch the stage, Plummer arrived at midnight to guard her. As Plummer sat by the stove watching Lucy pack, Vedder tiptoed up the back stairs, swung open the door, and pointed a pistol at him. "Your time is come," the gambler said, and quickly fired twice. Both shots missed, but when Plummer fired back, he hit Vedder.

Mortally wounded, Vedder fled down the stairs, collapsed, and drew his final breath. Lucy dashed into the street, crying hysterically that the marshal had killed her husband.

Arrested, Plummer was tried in a sensational case that went twice to the California Supreme Court before he was finally convicted of second-degree murder. Sentenced to ten years at San Quentin Prison, he began serving on February 22, 1859. Local residents immediately petitioned the governor for a pardon. He had acted in self-defense, they claimed. This support of Plummer's innocence bore the signatures of more than a hundred officials of two counties. Governor John Weller immediately granted a pardon, but instead of exonerating Plummer, he chose to cite the less controversial grounds of "imminent dangers of death from Consumption." Freed on August 16, 1859, he had spent a mere six months behind bars.

Returning to Nevada City, working at the bakery, he became quite a customer to the many brothels of the settlement. Though he did his best to behave like a miner—jingling ore samples in his pockets and supervising work at his claims—he could not shake his lawman ways. Soon, he made a successful citizen's arrest of San Quentin escapee "Ten Year" Smith.

But soon penniless and depressed, he joined a small gang of stagecoach bandits. In one robbery, the stage driver avoided being held up but identified Plummer as part of the gang. Standing trial for attempted robbery, Plummer was acquitted due to lack of evidence.

But trouble became his middle name when Plummer brawled with a man over the affections of a "painted lady." Plummer shot the man on October 27, 1861. He immediately surrendered himself to police, who locked him in a cell. One version of the story reports that the police agreed Plummer had acted in self-defense but feared his prison record would prevent a fair trial. They strongly suggested he leave the area and then allowed him to walk away from jail. Another version of the story suggests that after his arrest, but before going to trial, Plummer bribed a jailer for his release. Either way, he escaped a noose—again.

THE OWL HOOT TRAIL

Smarter than he looked—which was considerable, it was said—Plummer scooted down the Owl Hoot Trail up to Oregon. Along the way, he met another bandit, Jim Mayfield. Being they were both wanted men, they cooked up a scheme together to avoid frontier justice in the form of a hangman's noose. Plummer and Mayfield sent word to a California newspaper that both of them had been hanged in Washington. The two outlaws were "good 'n' dead." The story made headlines, and the public, along with Plummer and Mayfield, breathed a big sigh of relief. Beer mugs were hoisted, banners were raised, and bands played.

Until they got off the stage and surprised everyone. People were not happy.

Within days, the men hightailed it to safer ground. Plummer landed, in 1862, in Lewiston, Washington Territory (Idaho), with a woman and her children in tow. The lawman side of Plummer wouldn't be silent—acting like one, he dissolved a lynch mob with an eloquent speech. While this was admirable, the pro-vigilante faction was upset. He didn't know it then, but a dinner-plate-sized bull's-eye had landed on his back.

Character is built on good deeds, and Plummer had none. In January 1862, working in a casino in Lewiston, he ran into a few old San Quentin cellmates and immediately formed a gang. The outlaw side of him robbed local families in the area's mining camps and targeted gold shipments from the mines.

At some point, Plummer abandoned his woman (and her three children), and she was forced to resort to prostitution. She finally died an alcoholic in one of the seedier brothels.

Roaming between Elk City, Florence, and Lewiston, Plummer robbed and pillaged at will. In Orofino, Idaho, he killed a saloon keeper who had kicked Plummer and his friends out of the saloon. When some of the saloon keeper's friends formed a lynch mob, Plummer hightailed it out of there and headed east to Montana.

YOU CAN'T GO HOME

Totally defeated, Plummer decided to return home to Maine. With the Missouri River frozen over, he was forced to wait until spring thaw. During this time, James Vail, who was founding a mission station—the Sun River Farm, a government ranch and Indian agency—approached Plummer. Vail was recruiting volunteers to help protect his family from Indian attacks. With only a long wait ahead of him, Plummer accepted the job, along with Jack Cleveland, a horse dealer Plummer had known in California.

While at the mission, both Plummer and Cleveland fell in love with Vail's attractive sister-in-law, Electa Bryan. Thirty-year-old Plummer proposed marriage, and she agreed. As gold had recently been discovered in nearby Bannack, Montana, Plummer decided to go there to try to earn enough money to support them both. Leaving Electa at the Sun River Farm, he left in January 1863. Cleveland followed.

BANNACK, MONTANA

Bannack, the most recent site of gold rush fever, was home to transient men, including Civil War deserters from both sides, river pirates, professional gamblers, outlaws, and villains. Lawlessness ran rampant. On January 14, 1863, Plummer sat warming himself at the fire in the Goodrich Hotel saloon when Jack Cleveland attempted to provoke a shootout. Even after Plummer fired a warning shot into the saloon ceiling, Cleveland would not back down. Plummer fired twice, hitting and killing Cleveland.

Eyewitnesses provided similar testimony during the trial: Cleveland had threatened Plummer. Following the code of justice at the mines (that self-defense was judged according to who went for a weapon first), a miners' jury "honorably acquitted" Plummer.

Again, Plummer escaped the noose.

Lawlessness in Bannack had reached epidemic proportions, and the citizens were tired of it. They held an election for sheriff, and two men ran—a butcher and Henry Plummer. The butcher won, but apparently the loss did not sit well with Plummer. His reckless temper let loose, Plummer went after the butcher with a shotgun. The butcher shot Plummer in the right arm, temporarily ruining his gun-fighting abilities. So, Plummer learned to shoot well with his left. When the new sheriff/former butcher heard this, he turned in his badge and left Bannack—which left Plummer to be elected sheriff on May 24, 1863. "No man," a *Sacramento Union* reporter stated, "stands higher in the estimation of the community than Henry Plummer." This man, depicted in early diaries and journals, was a far cry from a bloodthirsty demon

First jail in Montana. In Bannack, since the ceiling was dirt and they could dig their way out, they were chained to the floor.
PHOTO COURTESY OF DANIEL TER-NEDDEN / WWW.GHOSTTOWNGALLERY.COM

addicted to robbery and mayhem. Instead, pioneers recalled seeing the "genteel-mannered" peace officer, fastidiously neat in his elegant overcoat, patrolling Bannack's streets at dawn.

On June 20, 1863, Plummer and Electa Bryan married and settled into their log home in Bannack. However, less than three months later, Electa left for her parents' home in Cedar Rapids, Iowa, and would never see Plummer again.

Two or More Sides to Every Story

Here's where stories about Plummer differ wildly.

One way Plummer is described is as a saint—someone who tried to stop the robberies, the drunkenness, the killings, the lootings. The other way is as the leader of the Innocents, a gang of over one hundred men who robbed, pillaged, and plundered at will. The group was so big, it was reported, that members resorted to using secret code words and hand signs to identify who was in the group.

Another version says this isn't so—no way could that many men control Montana. No way. As sheriff, after settling his bride into their log home at Bannack, Plummer convinced citizens that they needed a jail, ending the practice of immediate hangings. He publicly stated that he would put an end to the vigilante hangings. With subscriptions of $2.50, which Plummer collected himself, he constructed the first jail in what is now Montana. He became so popular that a Bannack political group recommended Plummer to be deputy US marshal.

The other side of the story is that the Innocents stepped up their efforts of robbing travelers from the gold-rich Montana camps. The few men who were caught thieving and were subsequently hanged on a gallows Plummer had built were *not* members of the infamous gang. Blatant killings and robberies continued, the local residents keeping quiet about identifying suspects for fear of retribution. Soon, Plummer expanded his operations to include Virginia City, Montana, when he was appointed deputy US marshal for the region of Idaho Territory in August 1863.

Some residents suspected Plummer of being the ringleader but were hesitant to come forward. But by December 1863, crime had reached an apex. Leading citizens of Virginia City, Bannack, and nearby Nevada City met in secret to form the Montana Vigilantes. Plummer was not included. But was Plummer actually a part of the murderous, cutthroat band of outlaws known as the Innocents, or was he simply a lawman stretched too thin?

Taking the law into their own hands, the Montana Vigilantes strung up a slew of outlaws within a few days. When one man, tight rope around his neck, pointed a finger toward Henry Plummer, saying he was the gang's leader, all hell broke loose, as they say. Shortly afterward, on January 10, 1864, after a heavy night of drinking, the Montana Vigilantes decided Plummer was guilty and tracked him down. It was reported that he was wrenched out of the arms of his loving wife and dragged to the gallows—which he had built. By this time, however, Electa had left.

Fifty to seventy-five men marched Plummer and two others to the gallows. The first two spouted curses until they were dead. Plummer, on the other hand, offered his captors a deal. He would tell the vigilantes where $100,000 worth of gold was buried if they would let him live.

Discussion followed, but they hanged him anyway. Of the three men strung up that night, only Henry Plummer was placed in a coffin; the others were wrapped in burlap. All of them were buried not in the town cemetery but in Hangman's Gulch, a hundred yards from the gallows.

AFTERWORD

On the side of Henry Plummer's innocence is the sobering fact that during their entire spree, the Montana Vigilantes never once encountered resistance from the Innocents. There was never a shootout or altercation between the two factions. It seemed as if Plummer's Gang never existed.

After Plummer's death, crime continued to rise even though the Vigilantes stayed busy, becoming ruthless. There is little evidence directly connecting Plummer with the gang other than the forced confession of an outlaw trying to save his own life. And Plummer's activities as an outlaw leader in Lewiston are in dispute since evidence was found that he was living in California for most of that time. Nevertheless, the fact of the matter is that William Henry Handy Plummer lived on both sides of the law, as did many people of that era.

So . . . which story do you want to believe? Guilty or not?

Chapter Three

Albert "Burt" Alvord:
Arizona's Practical Joker

Our bodies have arrived. Don't I look like myself?
—Burt Alvord

"Got me a great idea, boys!" Burt Alvord leaned forward, one elbow on the table, a beer glass in the other hand. He eyed his partners, Billy Stiles, Matt Burts, and Bill Downing, then dropped his voice to a husky whisper. "Train. We gonna rob us a train."

Billy flashed a wide grin under his handlebar mustache. "Hell, yeah." He held up a beer mug and clinked it against Burt's, then thudded against the chair back. "But we can't."

Alvord cocked his head. "Why not?"

"Dammit. 'Cause you're the gall darn marshal of Willcox."

What certainly seemed like a good idea at the time worked out moderately well. Alvord wasn't known for his high IQ or school learning, of which he had none. But he was likeable with a usual sense of cheerfulness and wicked sense of humor. He was a popular man around Cochise County, Arizona Territory, during the 1890s, working for a time as deputy for Cochise County sheriff John Slaughter. Supposedly Slaughter said Alvord didn't know the meaning of the word "fear," among many others. His interests seem to have been beer, poker, horses, guns, and practical jokes.

EARLY LIFE

Born in Plumas County, California, in 1867, Albert "Burt" W. Alvord moved with his family to various boomtowns throughout southern California and Arizona. His father, a New York native, mining mechanic, and prospector, eventually came to hold public offices such as constable and justice of the peace in several of the places where the family lived. They moved to Tombstone in 1879 when Alvord was twelve. His love of horses found him working at the O.K. Corral. At times he claimed to have witnessed the now-famous shootout there, but the boastings of an impressionable teenager remain unsubstantiated, although logically he might have been telling the truth.

BECOMING A LAWMAN

History could have easily forgotten Burt Alvord, except for the fact he had gained favor with Cochise County sheriff John Slaughter and the Alvord-Stiles Gang was the most notorious group of thugs in Arizona. Despite, and possibly because of, Alvord's reputation for frequenting saloons and participating in and/or causing minor skirmishes, Slaughter hired him as Cochise County deputy in 1886. He was reportedly "not noble, temperate, far seeing, or unselfish." However, he did manage to capture or kill several rustlers and outlaws between 1886 and 1889.

His alcoholism grew and his lawman image suffered. Not only did he continue to frequent saloons, he began associating with gamblers and known outlaws. In 1889, Sheriff Slaughter reprimanded him. Burt Alvord immediately resigned. The 1890s found him working as a lawman in southern Arizona boomtowns such as Fairbank, Pearce, and Willcox.

Former Cochise County deputy sheriff, Burt Alvord, in Yuma Prison, 1904.
AUTHOR'S COLLECTION

WHAT A GREAT IDEA!

It was in Willcox, in the late 1890s, that he concocted an idea to rob the Southern Pacific train. As marshal of the town, hired because of his reputation as a Tombstone "bad boy," no one would suspect him of such treachery. Lawmen were woefully underpaid, so robbery plans and alibis were hatched. The evening came when Alvord, along with drinking partners Billy Stiles, well-known cattleman Bill Downing, and Matt Burts sat playing poker in the back room at Schwertner's Saloon. The saloon's waiter routinely brought in rounds of drinks, returning with empty glasses, loudly telling the rest of the patrons that a serious poker game was going on and the door was to be closed at all times—do not disturb.

The ruse worked. No one noticed the four men wiggling out the side window, mounting their horses, and disappearing into the dark. No one noticed the four returning an hour later, their stash of valuables well hidden. After the robbery, the train engineer backed the locomotive into Willcox, sounding the alarm. Someone suggested they interrupt the constable playing cards at Schwertner's Saloon. After much consideration, they did.

Alvord reacted with alarm and dismay. "Great Scott!" Immediately, he pointed at his three fellow robbers. "I need volunteers for a posse. You, you, and you." To all within earshot, he declared, "We've got to run down those nefarious scallywags," and the posse galloped off into the night.

The next morning, no one was more disappointed than Burt Alvord, arriving back in town totally dejected, claiming that the posse, despite their best efforts at keeping eyes glued to the trail, had lost the culprits. A few eyebrows raised and rumors floated around town. Could he, the marshal, have been the ringleader? Alvord tried to defuse the gossip by claiming everyone knew he was too dumb to pull off such a clever caper. In all the chronicles of train robberies in the Old West, this was the only time the robbers and the posse chasing them were one and the same.

By the late 1890s, Tombstone had faded as a mining mecca. Speculators moved up the road to Pearce, taking some buildings from Tombstone with them.

Turned to Ranching?

A big, strapping, swarthy-looking fellow, Alvord married Lola Ochoa in 1896, bought a ranch near Pearce, Arizona, and tried to settle down. Once again, he was appointed a sheriff's deputy.

He kept his nose clean for about two years until his father died in 1899. Shortly afterward, he resigned, giving no reasons.

Again giving no reasons, he left his wife and returned to a life of crime.

BACK TO TRAIN ROBBING

Alvord's train robbing and law enforcement days were just getting started. It was hard to find good, reliable help, and Burt Alvord fit the bill. Hired as a lawman in Willcox, he hired Billy Stiles and Bill Downing as deputies. Conspiring to take advantage of his newfound legitimacy as a law enforcer, Alvord gathered local cowboys—including Matt Burts, brothers George and Louis Owen, and "Three Fingered Jack" Dunlop—to rob trains. Dunlop—who also went by Jack, John, or Jesse Dunlop or John Patterson—had been released from prison in 1895 and joined the "Black Jack" Christian Gang, but he began riding with Alvord shortly afterward.

Alvord's gang's first official train robbery took place at midnight in Cochise, Arizona, on September 11, 1899, when members Matt Burts and Billy Stiles, who were constables or deputies at this time, held up a Southern Pacific Express. Their plan: rob the car while it sat at the station. With people milling around, gathering to welcome the train, the outlaws blending in with the crowd and, if need be, using them as human shields, would work. And Alvord suspected the express car would be carrying the US Army's payroll for the soldiers stationed at Fort Huachuca.

The men detached the car containing the money, then opened the safe with dynamite and escaped with a bit over ten thousand dollars. They escaped into the Chiricahua Mountains with Sheriff Scott White and posse on their trail. As marshal, Alvord and his men led another posse to chase those robbers and, of course, found nothing.

On February 15, 1900, Burt Alvord, Billy Stiles, "Three Fingered Jack" Dunlop, Matt Burts, and Bravo Juan Tom Yoas robbed a train at Fairbank, Arizona, which served the dwindling town of Tombstone. However, well-known lawman Jeff Davis Milton was working as a guard on the train. A gunfight began, resulting in Milton shooting buckshot into Dunlop, wounding Juan Yoas. Milton was badly wounded in the right arm, and the gang fled.

Dunlop was hit in the stomach by eleven shotgun pellets, and Yoas was hit in the rear. The five outlaws split up, planning to meet outside Contention City, Arizona. Dunlop fell from his horse only a few miles from the robbery and lay there for fourteen hours before a posse found him. Taken to Tombstone where he confirmed the suspicion that Alvord's gang had backed the robbery, he gave an interview to *The Prospector* before dying on February 24, 1900. Dunlop was buried near the graves of Tom and Frank McLaury and Billy Clanton in Tombstone's Boot Hill.

THE GANG'S DOWNFALL

Armed with Dunlop's confession, lawmen arrested the Owen brothers, Bob Brown, Bill Downing, Billy Stiles, Matt Burts, and Burt Alvord. Stiles turned state's evidence, confessing he and Burts had committed the Cochise robbery and that Alvord and Downing had helped plan it. Released, Stiles went to Tombstone and busted Alvord out of jail.

This would be the downfall of the gang—but not the end of Burt Alvord and Billy Stiles. They continued to rob, pillage, and swindle in true Wild West fashion. In 1901, Alvord and Billy Stiles were captured but somehow managed to escape. Later that year, Alvord was captured and taken to Tombstone. Partner Billy Stiles rode into town and shot the deputy on duty in the foot, allowing Alvord and twenty-four other prisoners to escape.

Always willing to make deals, in 1902 Alvord contracted with Arizona Rangers captain Burton C. Mossman. If Alvord would help capture Mexican bandit Augustine Chacon, a notorious thief, then Alvord would receive a share of the reward money and a reduced sentence in exchange. Fast forward a few months.

Alvord found the bandit. Chacon was convicted of murder and hanged in Solomonville, Arizona. Shortly afterward, Alvord decided not to surrender after all, thinking hanging was his fate also. He went into hiding.

Burt Alvord's life became one of cat and mouse. Pursued by the Arizona Rangers, Alvord and Stiles were at last captured in December 1903, but they again managed to escape.

A JOKER

In addition to robbing trains, practical jokes were another of Alvord's specialties. One time he and a crony, Matt Burts, were visiting Bisbee, Arizona, when Alvord dreamed up another brilliant idea. "Let's fake our deaths," he says to outlaw partner Burts. "We'll send two bodies back to Tombstone and in a telegram we'll say it's us."

"Brilliant!" Matt replied.

They sent a telegram to Tombstone, announcing, "The bodies of Burts and Alvord will be arriving on the Bisbee stage this afternoon." Understandably, Tombstone's citizens were thrilled to learn these miscreants had finally been killed. Glasses were raised and much beer was consumed in their honor.

Then two events took place. Shortly after receiving the bodies, Tombstone's undertaker quickly declared that the dead men were not gringos like Alvord and Burts, but were, in fact, Mexicans. Then the live men arrived in town the next day, stepped off the coach, and grinned widely. They proclaimed, "Our bodies have arrived. We never go anywhere without 'em." It is unclear if the two Mexicans had been killed by the outlaws or were simply dug up.

A BOXING MATCH MADE IN . . . HEAVEN?

Boxing and wrestling were two of the most popular sports in the mining camps, and there was always a lot of money in the purse for the winner. Alvord figured making money like this would be

Tombstone 1881 grew from a tent city to over 7,000.
PHOTO BY C. S. FLY, CIRCA 1881, AUTHOR'S COLLECTION

easier than robbing trains. He partnered with a bold little Irishman named Biddy Doyle, an ex-soldier, ex-boxer, ex-wrestler, and fellow practical joker, someone Alvord fully understood. The men planned to relieve Bisbee's good citizens of some of their hard-earned cash by staging a wrestling match. Alvord and Doyle devised a way to have the outcome determined beforehand.

Doyle found a shill who would promote the fight. Then he contracted with a short but burly Cornish miner from the Copper Queen Mine to be his opponent. The miner agreed, for a goodly stipend, to take a fall. Bets were quickly made that the strapping Cornish miner would make mush out of the scrawny Irishman. Odds sailed to 20 to 1 against Doyle. This was to be no ordinary wrestling match.

Looking for the perfect arena, Doyle decided on a soft place for the actual wrestling site—a mule manure pile at the foot of the Copper Queen Mine located at the bottom of Tombstone Canyon. Alvord bet all their cash on Doyle to win. They stood to make a handsome profit if things went according to plan. They didn't, exactly. Perhaps a rehearsal or two would have helped.

A large crowd of sporting men arrived from Tombstone. Bisbee miners, businessmen, ranchers, and other spectators gathered. Anticipation built into a frenzy as the contestants were introduced. The match began with Doyle and the Cornishman warily stalking each other. Suddenly, Doyle maneuvered behind his opponent, pulled him to the ground, and pushed his face into the manure. The big man meekly surrendered.

While the spectators were momentarily stunned, Alvord decided that leaving town in a hurry was a good idea. He grabbed the purse containing several hundred dollars. He and Doyle sprinted to their horses and galloped away.

Returning to Tombstone, Alvord and Doyle bellied up to the bar in a saloon on Allen Street to celebrate their marvelous prank on the folks in Bisbee. Tombstone's newspaper took issue and chastised the two "bad boys" for tarnishing the town's good reputation. Not men to stay out of trouble, Alvord, with Billy Stiles by his side, ended up in the Tombstone jail once more. They escaped on December 15, 1903, and fled to Mexico, but Alvord would soon find himself back in jail. Once again, he escaped. Exasperated Arizona Rangers pursued Alvord and Stiles into Mexico and caught them riding near the village of Naco, on February 17, 1904. Both outlaws were wounded and finally surrendered.

ARRESTED AND JAILED

Because he was popular among the authorities, Alvord was charged with "interferring [*sic*] with United States mails" instead of train robbery, which would have meant death (a law passed in 1889). Alvord went to the Yuma Territorial Prison and remained there until 1906.

Following his release in 1906, Stiles and Alvord were still at it, according to a letter by Arizona Ranger H. H. McPhaul dated

July 2 of that year. He warned authorities that the duo, lurking "near the Mexican line south of Yuma," intended to rob a train "on the Southern Pacific system." The tip-off? The men were planning on placing water kegs along their escape route, intending to hold up "a train during the hot weather and with the aid of the water kegs and avoid any party sent after them," informants told McPhaul.

From here, reports vary as to Burt Alvord's remaining years. Some swear he changed his life around in 1906, sailing to Central America. Others report seeing him working as a canal employee in 1910. Yet others report he spent years roaming around South America, and after some time in Brazil, contracted fever in Barbados and died in 1910. Knowing Albert "Burt" W. Alvord, they could all be true.

AFTERWORD
According to historian David Leighton, Alvord Road in Tucson, Arizona, is named for the Practical Joker of Arizona.

CHAPTER FOUR

William (Billy) Larkin Stiles:
Better Criminal Than Lawman

BILLY STILES WOULD'VE BEEN SMARTER TO REMAIN AN OUTLAW. Certainly he'd been shot at a number of times during his various robberies, but other than being grazed a time or two, he was never actually wounded. He'd spent much of his early days as a train robber, bank robber, and killer. And partnering with law-man/outlaw Burt Alvord was a smart move for him. Together, they became Arizona's most feared and notorious pair of thugs. If Stiles had remained an outlaw, there's no telling how long he'd have lived.

But, like a chameleon, he turned from outlaw to lawman whenever the mood struck him. In his twenties and early thirties, he served twice as an Arizona deputy sheriff. When he moved to Humboldt County, Nevada, he pinned on a deputy's badge—that's where he made his fatal mistake.

EARLY LIFE

Born William Larkin Stiles in Casa Grande, Arizona, in 1871, not much is known about Stiles's early life. Rumors and specula-tion abound that he killed his father when he was twelve, but this tidbit has never been proven. Growing up near Casa Grande, at a young age Stiles struck out on his own, turning to hunting for elusive gold and silver. He also cowboyed in the nearby Superstition Mountains.

FORMING THE ALVORD-STILES GANG

Apparently prospecting and branding cattle didn't prove to be as lucrative as Stiles had imagined. He wanted more. Perhaps robbing trains would bring in gold—gold he didn't have to dig for. By the time his twenty-eighth birthday rolled around, Billy Stiles had joined forces with notorious outlaw Burt Alvord. Together they formed the Alvord-Stiles Gang, creating the most feared late nineteenth-century group of thugs in Arizona. Together, they planned and executed train robberies, becoming adept at escaping.

Their first known attempted robbery was of the Southern Pacific Railroad in Cochise, Arizona, in 1899. Despite careful planning, the robbery went awry. Their efforts netted nothing but capture. Arrested, they blamed each other for the failure. They pointed fingers at each other, questioned each other's intelligence, and ended up in separate cells. Soon, Alvord was set free. But Stiles couldn't seem to catch a break. Even his wife testified against him in court. Anger faded with time. The proverbial fences mended, Alvord soon broke his partner out of jail by tying up the jailer, taking the keys, and freeing Stiles.

The two disappeared from the area.

BECOMING A DEPUTY SHERIFF

In 1899 Stiles and Alvord returned to Willcox, Arizona, where Alvord became Cochise County sheriff and town marshal. Alvord immediately appointed Stiles—who was Pearce, Arizona's deputy constable—as his deputy. Even though they wore badges, their pay bordered on pitiful to nothing. Often the only pay they received was a percentage of the bounty placed on criminals' heads when they arrested them. Another duty was to collect taxes, and for their efforts, they kept part.

When Billy Stiles died, he went by the name Larkin.
HUMBOLDT STAR, DECEMBER 7, 1908 EDITION, AUTHOR'S COLLECTION

BECOMING AN OUTLAW—AGAIN

To supplement their meager earnings, they moonlighted as out-laws (as did more than one other sheriff). On September 11, 1899, the Alvord-Stiles Gang, which included partners "Three Fingered Jack" Dunlop, Bravo Juan Tom Yoas, Matt Burts, and brothers George and Louis Owen, robbed the Southern Pacific just as it was pulling into Cochise, ten miles west of Willcox.

Billy Stiles and Matt Burts climbed aboard the westbound train. One of them held a gun to the engineer and fireman, while the other uncoupled the engine and express car from the rest of the train. They ordered the engineer to take the train a few miles down the track. At a certain point, they climbed off the car, picking up a cache of hidden dynamite. They blew up the entire express car along with the Wells Fargo safe. Stiles and Burts made off with loot estimated between $3,000 and $300,000 in gold. They loaded the booty onto horses and rode back to Willcox.

The engineer backed his train into Willcox and sounded an alarm. When told of the robbery, town marshal Burt Alvord, sitting in the back room of Schwertner's saloon playing poker with his gang, jumped to his feet. He immediately appointed his pals to be deputies and members of the posse. After a long night of searching, a frustrated Alvord reported he had failed to find the nefarious outlaws.

Known as an expert tracker, Billy Stiles worked for a while under Cochise County sheriff John Slaughter.

FAIRBANK, ARIZONA, ROBBERY

Feeling good about their 1899 train robbery, Burt Alvord and Billy Stiles planned another heist. This time they let "Three Fingered Jack" Dunlop, Bravo Juan Yoas, Bob Brown, and the Owen brothers rob a train in Fairbank. Although Billy Stiles was a gang member, he was not part of the robbery. But he certainly was part of the project.

The plan was to look like drunken cowboys mingling among the crowd. They'd use passengers and people milling around as human shields in case gunfire erupted. It did. They hadn't figured on legendary gunfighter and shotgun messenger Jefferson Davis Milton being in the express car. The moment the outlaws opened the car, they shot. Their lever-action Winchesters shattered Milton's left arm, severing the artery. While shooting, Milton wrapped his wound and slid between two crates, saving his life. He grabbed the Wells Fargo shotgun and pelted Dunlop with eleven shotgun pellets in his stomach, a fatal wound. Yoas was shot in his rear. The gang scattered, planning to meet up later in Contention, Arizona.

Some people in Willcox thought Alvord was the leader, but he countered he wasn't smart enough to plan something as complex as a train robbery. Since Alvord was the only one who knew where the gold from the last robbery was hidden, dissension fomented among the gang. Tired of the games, Billy Stiles, a pugnacious and treacherous man, broke under pressure, thinking he wouldn't get his fair share, and confessed in exchange for his freedom.

With Stiles's testimony, the gang was locked up in Tombstone's County Jail. Apparently changing his mind, and perhaps feeling a bit guilty about Alvord, on April 8, 1900, Billy Stiles went to visit his partner. He held a gun on Deputy Marshal George Bravin, demanding the release of all the prisoners. When Bravin didn't comply immediately, Stiles shot him in the foot, taking off two toes. Twenty-four prisoners, including Alvord, escaped.

Early photo of railway station in Fairbank, Arizona.
AUTHOR'S COLLECTION

TO MEXICO!

The marauding duo of Stiles and Alvord vanished into Mexico until 1902. At that time, ex–Texas Ranger and Arizona Ranger captain Burt Mossman went undercover, asking for their help to capture Mexican bandit Augustine Chacon. In return, they were to surrender to authorities and receive light sentences. They rode near the town of Naco, Mexico, where they apprehended Chacon. According to Arizona historian Marshall Trimble, Chacon was "one of the last of the hard-riding desperados who rode the owl-hoot trail in Arizona around the turn of the century." He was considered extremely dangerous, having killed about thirty people. He was hanged that same year.

Even though the jail terms for Stiles and Alvord were short, they broke out of the Tombstone jail again, this time digging through a wall and tunneling their way out. Eventually, Alvord was captured and sent to Yuma Territorial Prison for two years. Stiles, seeing the writing on the wall, so to speak, surrendered to Mossman and agreed to serve in the Arizona Rangers in exchange for jail time. The roster of Arizona Rangers shows that Stiles was thirty-two when he enlisted. He did, however, turn back to lawlessness soon after.

Rightfully, the Arizona Rangers were not thrilled to have an outlaw as one of their own, particularly one of considerable notoriety. They trailed Stiles and Alvord for a number of months down into Mexico, locating them in February 1904. Not willing to go peacefully, Stiles and his partner shot it out with the Rangers. Alvord was hit twice and surrendered, but Stiles took a bullet in his arm and still managed to escape.

Alvord spent two years, from 1904 to 1906, in the Yuma, Arizona, Territorial Prison.

While his partner was busy sitting in jail, Billy Stiles made his way across the Pacific to Asia, where he stayed for a few years in China and the Philippines. Returning to the United States, he ended up in Nevada, changing his name and becoming a deputy sheriff in Humboldt County. He then went by William Larkin, substituting his middle name for his last name.

On December 5, 1908, Billy Larkin Stiles rode to the Riley Ranch on the Kings River, about ninety miles north of Winnemucca, Nevada. John Saval, a prominent sheepman, accompanied Larkin to serve a court summons on Charley Barr, wanted in connection with a murder. After a leisurely lunch at the ranch house, Larkin walked toward the barn, warrant in hand. Saval remained behind, putting on overshoes. About halfway between the house and the barn, Barr stepped out and fired three shots, each striking Larkin. Larkin returned fire but hit nothing.

Larkin died in the dirt. He was thirty-seven.

Charley Barr rushed into the ranch house, grabbed all the guns there, then selected the best saddle horse on the ranch and turned out all the other horses. He galloped away toward the Oregon line.

Afterword

At the coroner's inquest, since Billy Stiles was using the last name Larkin, many were confused about whom exactly Charley Barr had killed. A woman claiming to be his sister-in-law finally appeared and said the dead man was definitely Billy Stiles. Later, the woman in question revealed herself to be Stiles's wife, whom he'd left several years earlier. Why the deceit? No one knows.

Charley Barr was indicted and tried for Stiles's murder, but in 1914 he was found not guilty. The jurors believed that because Stiles had threatened Barr on previous occasions, Barr had acted in self-defense.

Buried at the Pioneer Cemetery on the north bank of the Humboldt River, William Larkin Stiles died a lawman. His grave is now unmarked. Later, his name was added to a plaque of Law Enforcement Memorial in Carson City, Nevada. His name is inscribed at the National Peace Officer Memorial in Washington, DC.

CHAPTER FIVE

John Joshua (J. J.) Webb:
Member of the Dodge City Gang

*From an officer to a felon's cell, from a felon's cell to the gallows
in thirty days.*

—CHICAGO TIMES, 1880

LAS VEGAS, NEW MEXICO, IN THE LATTER PART OF THE NINE-
teenth century was a wild and woolly place, full of thieves, con
men, prostitutes, opportunists, and men of questionable morals.
Since 1822, Las Vegas had been a major stop on the Santa Fe
Trail and had seen its share of characters. The Gallinas River
divided the town into East and West, each reporting 1,500 citizens in 1880. The East called itself "New Town," the West "Old
Town," being the older, more established side. The town today is
still referred to as East or West Las Vegas, and yes, there remains
an unspoken rivalry.

In 1879, John Joshua (J. J.) Webb rode into town. Already
there were Hyman P. "Hoodoo Brown" Neill and Doc Holliday,
along with saloon owner William Goodlett; city marshal Joe
Carson; outlaw "Mysterious Dave" Mather; hard cases "Dirty
Dave" Rudabaugh, Selim K. "Frank" Cady, William P. "Slap Jack
Bill" Nicholson, John "Bull Shit Jack" Pierce, and Jordan L. Webb

(no relation to J. J.); and a slew of other rough-and-tumble men, gunfighters, and gamblers.

What did these men have in common? All had lived in Dodge City at some point, and all were of questionable moral fiber. They called themselves the Dodge City Gang. The group managed to get members or friends into local law enforcement positions, the idea being that their actions would control the gambling establishments and rake in substantial profits. The gang, in control of a criminal cartel, thumbed their noses at the real law. For two years, members of the gang participated in several stagecoach and train robberies, organized cattle rustling, and were said to have been responsible for multiple murders and lynchings.

While there was "law" in Las Vegas, mostly on the West side, the East was governed by the gang. The gang's leader, Hoodoo Brown, served as justice of the peace and in 1880 appointed Webb as town marshal. Soon afterward, he was made an official member of the Dodge City Gang.

The gang had ruled East Las Vegas since the coming of the railroad, and it appeared they couldn't be stopped. But two factors led to the gang's demise. First, death and destruction became so rampant that by early 1880, the townspeople put together their own form of frontier justice. One hundred men, armed with rifles, shotguns, and pistols, made it known that they were fed up with the killings, the corruption, the "wildness." When the gang saw for themselves that the vigilantes meant business, they scattered. Peace reigned over Las Vegas.

The second factor in their demise was Webb's shooting of Mike Kelliher.

THE KILLING OF MIKE KELLIHER
John Joshua Webb testified about the March 2, 1880, shooting: "I was serving as a police officer when I demanded his gun. I killed Kelliher to save my life. I was told that he was going to kill me and his actions led me to believe that he would. I thought Kelliher

J. J. Webb was an instrumental part of the Dodge City Gang.
AUTHOR'S COLLECTION

a dangerous man is the reason that I wished to disarm him" (*Las Vegas Optic*, March 10, 1880).

Webb was more than a police officer—he was city marshal. He stated that he and Doc Holliday had been at Goodlett and Roberts' Saloon in Las Vegas, passing an evening playing cards, when Michael Kelliher, a freighter, rancher, and former Chicago policeman who was rumored to have a considerable amount of cattle-buying money on him, entered. Webb was given the cue that Kelliher was heeled—armed with a pistol—violating city ordinances.

"I won't be disarmed. Everything goes," Kelliher said when Webb asked for the weapon.

Kelliher reached for his gun.

"I then shot him twice." Webb shrugged, explaining his innocence at his hearing. In reality, he shot three times, striking Kelliher twice in the chest and once in the head.

Although the shooting was seemingly justified, rumors spread that Hoodoo Brown, justice of the peace and leader of the infamous gang, had information that Kelliher had $1,900 on his person and had sent Webb to take it. Upon hearing about the shooting, Hoodoo, acting as coroner, arrived immediately and impaneled a coroner's jury of his friends. They ruled that "the deceased came to his death from a pistol at the hands of J. J. Webb, being an officer in the discharge of his duty, and the killing was justifiable and necessary under the circumstances."

Was it possible that Webb was set up by Hoodoo and John "Dutchy" Schunderberger, a strapping young fellow who was handy with his fists? Dutchy served as Hoodoo's chief clerk and bodyguard, and left with Hoodoo soon after the incident. It's assumed that the pair was motivated by both greed and a desire to get back at Webb for some underhanded activities. Webb insisted after the shooting and again at the hearing that he'd been given the impression that Kelliher wanted to kill him. As he'd stated earlier, it was a kill-or-be-killed situation. Turns out Kelliher had more money on him than Webb had been told, and Hoodoo made off with the bulk of it.

The "law" in East Las Vegas did not charge Webb with Kelliher's killing, however; Kelliher's brother rode into town looking for him. Upon hearing about the shooting, he went across the river to West Las Vegas, where a grand jury was in session at the courthouse. They investigated, then heard evidence that Kelliher had been the victim of a conspiracy to obtain his money. On March 4, the jury quickly returned indictments against Webb, charging him with first-degree murder, and charging Hoodoo with larceny. Webb was arrested.

J. J. Webb was friends with "Dirty Dave" Rudabaugh, whom he once arrested.
COURTESY ALBUQUERQUE POLICE MUSEUM

SO LONG, HOODOO

Webb was taken into custody, but Hoodoo had vanished. The *Las Vegas Optic* reported that Hoodoo and Dutchy had boarded a train that night and had last been seen the next morning north in Otero, a railroad construction camp one hundred miles up the line near present-day Raton, where they had breakfast. On the way, according to the article, Hoodoo had shown a large roll of greenbacks to the conductor. Later, he gave Dutchy $150 and the two parted, Dutchy heading north and Hoodoo east into Kansas.

With Hoodoo gone, the back of the Dodge City Gang was broken. Webb was sentenced to hang. More than likely it was the general dislike of the Dodge City Gang that weighed more on his conviction than his actual guilt in this particular instance. Webb requested a new trial, but the motion was denied.

On March 12, 1880, the *Chicago Times* wrote of Webb: "From an officer to a felon's cell, from a felon's cell to the gallows in thirty days." Later, attorneys managed to get his sentenced reduced to life.

EARLY YEARS

John Joshua Webb was born on Valentine's Day 1847, in Keokuk County, Iowa, the seventh of twelve children of William Webb Jr. and Innocent Blue Brown Webb. Webb and his family moved to Nebraska in 1862, and later to Osage City, Kansas. Webb headed west on his own in 1864, working as a buffalo hunter and miner along the way.

In his thirty-five years, Webb would distinguish himself as a skilled army scout, lawman, and gunfighter. Doing odd jobs, he wandered from Deadwood, South Dakota, to Cheyenne, Wyoming, and eventually to Dodge City, Kansas. During this time he worked as a buffalo hunter and miner. The Ford County (Kansas) Census of 1875 listed Webb as a twenty-eight-year-old teamster.

Webb was deputized to ride in several posses during his time in Dodge City. In September 1877, Webb went to Lakin, Kansas, with Ford County sheriff Charlie Bassett and under-sheriff Bat Masterson in pursuit of the Sam Bass Gang, who were heading south toward Texas. Bass and his men had recently robbed a Union Pacific train of sixty thousand dollars at Big Springs, Nebraska. Bass's gang's expected route home would lead them through southwest Kansas. The search was unsuccessful. Although Bass eluded the posse this time, he met his death the next year in Round Rock, Texas.

Newly promoted Ford County sheriff Bat Masterson deputized Webb again in pursuit of a six-member gang who had robbed the westbound train at Kinsley, Kansas. On January 29, 1878, the posse took off and caught two of the gang members within days of the holdup. One of those outlaws was "Dirty Dave" Rudabaugh. "Dirty Dave" was an appropriate moniker for a man who rarely bathed and even more infrequently changed his clothes. Upon capture, Rudabaugh went for his gun but was overwhelmed by Webb and disarmed. Also arrested was Edgar West. The other four accomplices were arrested several days later. Rudabaugh informed on his cohorts, received a prison sentence, but was later released. Rudabaugh piously pledged "to earn his living on the square," but he soon drifted to New Mexico and resumed his outlaw ways.

FROM LAWMAN TO FELON

Newspapers in Dodge City depict Webb as a well-respected member of the community, serving as a businessman and lawman during this time. However, most historians believe he was a mercenary for the Atchison, Topeka and Santa Fe Railway in its battle against the Denver and Rio Grande Railroad for right-of-way through Raton Pass. Both railroads had extended lines into Trinidad, Colorado, and the pass was the only access to continue on to New Mexico. There was much legal maneuvering and even threatened violence between rival gangs of railroad workers. To break the impasse, Atchison, Topeka and Santa Fe hired a number of local gunfighters in February 1878. Faced with this threat, and running out of money, the Denver and Rio Grande was forced to cede the pass to its rival.

Early in 1879, Webb opened the Lady Gay Saloon in Dodge City. That summer, he was among the Dodge City gunmen hired by the Santa Fe Railroad in its fight with the Denver and Rio Grande for possession of the Royal Gorge in Colorado, the only railroad gateway to booming Leadville. While in the service of the railroad, the newspaper biography said Webb conducted himself in a "praiseworthy manner" by refusing an $8,000 bribe offered by the rival railroad. The Santa Fe Railroad gave him a $500 reward for his faithfulness and unflinching courage.

There, Webb came into contact with several notable personalities of the Old West, including Wyatt Earp and Doc Holliday.

However, with a silver strike in Leadville, the two railroads' struggles stirred once again. Now both railroads were competing to put track along the narrow Royal Gorge. The Denver and Rio Grande hired its own gunfighters, so the Atchison, Topeka and Santa Fe decided to strengthen its forces. On March 20, 1879, the railroad hired Masterson to put together a group of gunmen. They had great success through early June 1879, but on June 10, the state Fourth Judicial Circuit ruled in favor of the Denver and Rio Grande, changing matters entirely. The war was essentially over with the Denver and Rio Grande in control of the Royal Gorge.

Las Vegas, New Mexico, began as a major stop on the Santa Fe Trail.
AUTHOR'S COLLECTION

From Dodge City to Las Vegas

With the conflict over, Webb left Dodge City, then followed the railroad down to Las Vegas, hiring on with the Adams Express Company as a special detective. Later that same year, he was involved in stagecoach and train robberies in the vicinity of the town. In short order, he met up with "Mysterious Dave" Mather (who claimed to be related to Cotton Mather, though the Mather family has denied kinship), Doc Holliday, Dirty Dave Rudabaugh, Wyatt Earp, and others. Within a short time, however, Webb was considered part of the Dodge City Gang.

Strangely, while the people of Dodge City always saw John J. Webb as an ace-high, law-abiding citizen, his time in Las Vegas has been categorized in a completely different light.

Webb's Almost Jail Break

After being found guilty of murdering Mike Kelliher, Webb sat in jail watching men he'd known—some he'd arrested—come and go, many staying. As a free man, Rudabaugh visited Webb many times, obviously forgiving Webb for arresting him two years earlier. On April 30, 1880, the jailer, Antonio Lino Valdez, did not hesitate to open the door and permit Rudabaugh and John Llewellyn, known as "Little Allen," to enter the jail's walled *placita*, the inner courtyard. This time proved fatal.

Rudabaugh handed the prisoner a newspaper. At that moment, Allen asked Valdez to hand him the keys to Webb's cell. When he said no, he would not, could not, Allen shot him. They grabbed the keys, tossed them into Webb's cell, then ran, shouting to Webb to free himself. Webb chose not to, instead remaining behind bars. Why, exactly, is anyone's guess.

As written in the *Las Vegas Daily Gazette* on April 4, 1880, "It was a bold and desperate attempt to liberate Webb, which failed on account of lack of nerve and courage on the part of the projectors. . . . How did they imagine that he should get out and escape on foot without arms. It was an ill-advised plan for their object and nervelessly executed. They made a good escape, however, and luckily for them met the mounted herders, otherwise the chances are that the party would have overhauled them, in which case it would be a dead sure thing they would have been captured."

A *Chicago Times* correspondent wrote: "Webb is a regular type of western bully, a big, burly coarse fellow, well fitted mentally and physical for the villainous part he took in the horrible affair (the killing of Mike Kelliher). He was rather a self-appointed officer, which position he was allowed to hold partly because his reckless and fearless habits made him a very good man in quieting disturbances."

WEBB'S FIRST REAL JAIL BREAK

On November 10, 1880, Webb, along with five other prisoners, picked the lock of their cell door during the night and walked out of the unlocked front door of the jail. Las Vegas newspapers speculated that the guards, perhaps, had been bribed.

The following day, the San Miguel County sheriff led a posse and found the six fugitives camped southeast of town. Everyone opened fire, killing two of the six. Webb and George Davis (charged with stealing mules) got away.

Meanwhile, Lincoln County sheriff Pat Garrett was leading a large posse in search of Billy the Kid. At daybreak on November 26, 1880, Garrett and his boys surrounded the Dedrick ranch house, hoping to find the Kid. Instead, they found Davis and Webb. Sheriff Garrett himself escorted the two back to Las Vegas.

On December 26, 1880, Sheriff Garrett brought Rudabaugh back to town, along with Billy the Kid and two other members of the gang. Rudabaugh was thrown into the same jail as Webb.

WEBB'S SECOND JAIL BREAK

Webb languished in jail over a year, then decided to break out. Working with Rudabaugh and five others, he escaped. The jailed prisoners who were left behind explained to officers that the escapees, using a knife and just the head of a pickax, had spent much of the night digging and cutting through the cement and heavy stones of the wall, dropping the debris silently onto soft mattresses. The smallest of the group, William Goodman, had squeezed through the 7" × 19" hole and was first out.

On December 4, 1881, the *Las Vegas Daily Gazette* reported, "When on the outside, it is supposed that they handed the pick out to Goodman so that he could break off a part of the stone and make the hole bigger. He did not succeed, however, and the others had to squeeze through the narrow place as best they could, one after the other." The other six, including Webb, were forced to remove their clothes before escaping. Once outside, they dressed and ran.

Later that same morning, a man who lived near the railroad tracks about two miles south of town noticed two men walking together down the tracks. Chains dangled from the legs of one of the men, Rudabaugh. John Joshua Webb and Dirty Dave Rudabaugh literally walked out of Las Vegas—forever.

In the same December 4, 1881, article, the *Las Vegas Daily Gazette* stated, "J. J. Webb was under sentence for life, but would have been pardoned by Lew Wallace just before the expiration of his term as Governor if it had not been that his term of office was so near a close."

Drifting, Webb returned to Kansas, where he took the name Samuel King and worked as a teamster. Somewhere along the line he moved on to Winslow, Arkansas, working for the railroad.

News of his death in 1882 arrived in a letter to the mayor of Dodge City and was published in the *Dodge City Times*:

Dear Sir: John J. Webb is dead. He died on the 12th inst. of smallpox in Winslow, Arkansas. He was there working for J. D. Scott & Co., on the St. L. & S.F. RR. He had the best attention and care, but there came a sudden change in the weather and I suppose he caught cold, and he died very sud-

denly. He was going under the name of Sam King, after he came here. You can tell the friends of his death.

[signed] J. A. Scott

John Joshua Webb never married.

Chapter Six

"Hoodoo Brown": Founder of the Dodge City Gang

Baddest Cowboy of Them All.
—Harold Thatcher, Las Vegas
Rough Rider Museum curator

After what seems to have been a mostly successful time running an opera company in Mexico with a friend, Hyman G. "Hoodoo Brown" Neill drifted to the town of Las Vegas, New Mexico. He soon ruled the place, already notorious as the most lawless in the West. In 1879, by means natural and/or supernatural, but none of them honest, Hoodoo was justice of the peace, mayor, and coroner of East Las Vegas.

A description of him appeared in a March 1880 article in the *Chicago Times*: "He is a tall, thin man, has light hair, small mustache, and a rakish look which is a terrible giveaway, and one would at once set him down as a desperate character, and a man to beware of." He recruited the "baddest" of the bad and soon commanded a formidable band of outlaws who enforced law and committed crimes as they saw fit. The group, known as the Dodge City Gang, included men with some of the most colorful names in the West, like "Mysterious Dave" Mather and "Dirty Dave"

Rudabaugh. Acting as Hoodoo's coroner's jury, they would decide which murders, including ones they committed, were homicide and which were self-defense.

According to Harold Thatcher, former curator of the Rough Rider Museum in Las Vegas, New Mexico, Hoodoo was "the baddest cowboy of them all." By the time Hoodoo arrived in Las Vegas in early 1879, the town was filled with murderers, thieves, con men, and men out to make a quick dollar. They all gave East Las Vegas a bad name. Las Vegas had grown into a major stop on the Santa Fe Trail beginning in 1822. Merchants, wares dealers, and immigrants, along with others, passed through town, all bringing their own sets of values and morals. Divided by the Gallinas River, Las Vegas separated into East and West early on. East, or "New Town," was filled with drifting cowboys, bunko artists,

Hoodoo Brown was rumored to dabble in the black arts which lead to his nickname.
AUTHOR'S COLLECTION

prostitutes, gamblers, and general riffraff. Businessmen and community leaders populated West Las Vegas, or "Old Town." In the 1880s, both sides sported about 1,500 people each. Together, the East and West made Las Vegas a good-sized Southwestern town.

By the time Hoodoo arrived, the place was already jumping. The railroad was coming. Supported by other recent immigrants to town, Hoodoo was quickly elected justice of the peace. Also serving as mayor and coroner, he gathered several former gunfighters he'd known from Kansas and formed a police force. These men were ironically called "peace officers," and they policed people new to town. Soon the officers showed their true colors and became known as the Dodge City Gang. The Gang included J. J. Webb as town marshal, along with Mysterious Dave Mather, Joe Carson, and Dirty Dave Rudabaugh as deputies and police officers.

HOODOO STARTS OUT AS A PRINTER'S DEVIL

Hoodoo hailed from a traditional Southern family from Lexington, Missouri. Not much is known about his early life, and his year of birth is estimated to be 1856. Hoodoo's father, Henry Alexander Neill, had come to Lexington from Lee County, Virginia, in the 1830s. He practiced law and would have joined the Confederacy when the Civil War began. However, he decided he could not disavow his oath to support the Constitution and ended up joining the Union. This choice, coupled with his wife's death, caused him to move his family to Warrensburg, Missouri, after the war.

As a teenager, Hoodoo became a printer's devil (printer's assistant). One day he was asked to retrieve rags needed to clean up a printing press. Obviously not satisfied with the job, instead of doing what was asked, young Hoodoo jumped onto a freight train passing by the back door of the office, saying he was leaving to "get your durn rags." He failed to return.

By 1872 he was hunting buffalo and hauling lumber from Russell, Kansas, to Dodge City. He was also known to be a small-time gambler and confidence man. Arrested a time or two on minor charges such as vagrancy, he drifted on to Colorado where he worked in the silver mines with a friend, then took off for Mexico where they formed a ragtag opera company for the edification of the villagers. Apparently, some "fleecing" of the villagers was in order, too.

Forms the Dodge City Gang

Returning to America, he rode into Las Vegas in 1879 and immediately created the Dodge City Gang. The members were rampantly corrupt. It is rumored that Hoodoo dabbled in the black arts when all else failed to take people's money. He was a successful and frequent conjure man, inspiring his nickname of Hoodoo.

From 1879 through 1880, Hoodoo led his gang in stagecoach and train robberies, murder, thievery, and municipal corruption. An article in the *Chicago Times* written by a Las Vegas correspondent in March 1880 describes Hoodoo's courtroom: "The novel way in which he always opened court contains a little grim humor and illustrates how law reigned here. He would seat himself and say, 'Myself and partner will now open court,' pointing to a large, double-barreled Winchester lying against the desk at his side."

The other side of Hoodoo as justice of the peace was reported in the *Las Vegas Gazette* on November 1, 1879: "Thursday evening a young man named Marshall, when settling his bill at the Parker house, had a dispute with [the boarding house manager] K. P. Brown, and invited him outdoors. On getting out, Marshall drew a pistol and stuck it in Brown's face. Brown returned to the office but could not get a pistol. Later in the evening Marshall was arrested and taken before Justice Neill [Hoodoo], who after hearing evidence, complimented both parties on their good looks and genteel appearance and advised them to divide the cost, which done, the case was dismissed."

In March 1880, the *Chicago Times* said of Hoodoo, "He has been in the western wilds for many years, and for a long time was one of the worst class of low gamblers. . . . When he came here, there was great hustle and bustle and excitement with building houses and railroads, and the roughs and gamblers being the only idle ones, had things pretty much their own way, and elected him justice of the peace and coroner. He conducted his business in a fearless manner, and rather won the admiration of the citizens, although they always mistrusted him."

Killing of Joe Carson and the "Hanging Windmill"

Four cowboys rode into town in January 1880, hell-bent on having a good time, letting off a little steam. They made their rounds of the many saloons and gambling halls, as well as the "houses of negotiated affections." According to the *Las Vegas Optic*, well heeled, they paraded up and down the streets and laughed at law officers who suggested they check their weapons until leaving town.

The group's leader, twenty-one-year-old Tom Henry, who had a "checkered past" in Texas, had reportedly come to the area to steal horses. By January 22, they had disturbed the peace by shooting their guns, drinking boisterously, and cursing everyone they met. Still well armed, the four roamed into the Close and Patterson Dance Hall in East Las Vegas.

Forty-year-old town marshal Joe Carson approached the men and asked them for their guns—only until they left town. They ignored the lawman, and he repeated the request. According to eyewitnesses, the answer was a barrage of profane insults, which turned into a barrage of bullets. Carson managed to pull his gun from his hip pocket and fire two shots before falling to the floor with nine bullets in his body.

Assistant town marshal "Mysterious Dave" Mather was standing nearby. He drew his gun and opened fire. The dance hall was riddled with at least forty shots. When the considerable smoke cleared, one of the cowboys lay dead, as did Marshal Carson. Another was down with a bullet through his middle but still alive.

Tom Henry, shot in the calf, limped outside, where he met the only one of his men not hurt. The two jumped on horses and galloped into the night, leaving behind their injured friend, who was immediately arrested and jailed.

Two weeks later, word arrived in Las Vegas that the wanted men were hiding out at a farmhouse near Mora, several miles northwest of town. It was rumored they were waiting for Tom Henry's leg to heal enough so they could skedaddle out of the country. On February 5, a posse comprised of J. J. Webb, Dave Rudabaugh, and others found the fugitives. After much posturing, the men agreed to surrender, but with the stipulation they would be protected from any mob violence in Las Vegas.

The posse agreed, and the fugitives were arrested. Interviewed by a *Las Vegas Optic* reporter, Henry, using third-person, explained his motives: "When a fellow of his disposition gets too much whisky on board, he lost control of himself and was driven to deeds, the enormity of which were not realized until more sober moments."

The posse may have promised protection from a frontier justice "necktie party," but it didn't prevent more than a hundred angry citizens from battering down the jail door, demanding the cell keys, and escorting all three dance hall shooters to the "hanging windmill" on the plaza. They dragged the men up to the windmill platform, put ropes around their necks, and then looped the ropes up over beams in the windmill's structure.

The first to be hanged was the man suffering from a belly wound. While he hung there, the other two were giving final statements when, according to reporters, the slain marshal's widow appeared in the crowd. She picked up a rifle and began shooting at the three men. General gunfire erupted as the mob followed her lead. When the smoke cleared for a second time, all three were dead. They were later placed in individual coffins and buried in a single grave.

A brief item in the *Las Vegas Optic* that same day said, "There is a petition in circulation to have the windmill torn down. It is too great a temptation." The windmill was indeed dismantled later that day, not only because it was a "temptation," but because it was a bad influence on the children of Las Vegas. The article goes on to explain, "Yesterday, boys were hanging dogs all over town and many a poor dog had his neck stretched just by force of example."

Several men hung from the windmill before it was torn down.
AUTHOR'S COLLECTION

The Killing of Mike Kelliher

The end of Gang rule was brought about by the March 2, 1880, unprovoked killing of Mike Kelliher, owner of three freighting teams and a ranch in the Dakotas. Kelliher and his friend, William Brickley, had camped outside of town but had spent all day chasing a string of horses that had escaped. Needing a cold beer and supper, the men walked into town. Kelliher had $2,115 in his pocket, not having the chance to deposit it in the bank that day.

Rumors flew, and Hoodoo knew within moments how much money Kelliher had on him. Kelliher and Brickley visited a dance hall in West Las Vegas and then crossed the bridge to enjoy some of the other nightlife. Before returning to camp around 3 a.m., the two stopped for a final drink at the Goodlett and Roberts Saloon, one of Hoodoo's favorite hangouts (William Goodlett was part of the Dodge City Gang). According to eyewitnesses, the two met a friend there, and about half an hour later, Deputy J. J. Webb entered, telling Kelliher to hand over his weapon since it was against town ordinances to carry guns in town. Kelliher refused. Webb shot three times, hitting Kelliher twice in the chest and once in the head.

Upon hearing about the shooting, Hoodoo, acting as coroner, arrived immediately and impaneled a coroner's jury of his friends. They ruled "the deceased came to his death from a pistol at the hands of J. J. Webb, being an officer in the discharge of his duty, and the killing was justifiable and necessary under the circumstances." Although the shooting was seemingly justified, rumors spread that Hoodoo had information that Kelliher had $1,900 on his person and had sent Webb to take it. Was it possible that Hoodoo set up Webb?

Hours after the shooting, Hoodoo asked the San Miguel County probate judge to appoint him Kelliher's estate administrator. Hoodoo said he had taken $1,900 from the body of the deceased during the inquest at the saloon. A question of bond arose, and while the judge was thinking, it was brought to light that Hoodoo had taken another $860 off Kelliher.

Not satisfied with the "investigation" and ruling, Brickley demanded better answers and a "real" court of law. On March 4, 1880, a grand jury, which was in session at the courthouse in West Las Vegas, investigated the shooting and heard Kelliher was the victim of a conspiracy to obtain his money. The jury charged Webb with first-degree murder and Hoodoo with larceny.

HOODOO TAKES OFF

But Hoodoo had vanished. The *Las Vegas Optic* on March 5 reported, "After the killing of Kelliher, the money in [Hoodoo's] possession, said to be $1950, instead of only $1090, as given to the reporters, fell into the hands of Neill [Hoodoo]. . . . The funeral expenses were borne and Neill put the rest of the money in his pockets and skipped for parts unknown."

The *Optic* also reported that Hoodoo and John "Dutchy" Schunderberger, a husky young man who was handy with his fists and who served as Hoodoo's chief clerk and bodyguard, had boarded a train that night. They were last seen the next morning north in Otero, a railroad construction camp one hundred miles up the line near present-day Raton, where they had breakfast. On the way, according to the *Optic's* article, Hoodoo had shown a large roll of greenbacks to the conductor. Later, he gave Dutchy $150, and the two parted, Dutchy heading north toward Alamosa, Colorado, and Hoodoo east into Kansas.

It was a good thing they left, because by the summer of 1880, the citizens of Las Vegas were fed up with Hoodoo's corruption and the lack of true law by the Dodge City Gang. A group of at least one hundred citizens banded together to form their own version of frontier justice. The men brought rifles, shotguns, and pistols, making clear to the riffraff that they would no longer tolerate bad behavior. They'd already hanged one man and would have hanged two more if Widow Carson hadn't shot them. Most of the Gang scattered.

TO HOUSTON

On March 8, 1880, the US marshal's office in Parsons, Kansas, received an urgent telegram from Las Vegas:

> *Arrest Hyman G. Neill, alias Hoodoo Brown, about six feet in height, light hair and mustache, weighs about 140, slim and active, blue eyes, dressed in plaid grey suit, going to Houston,*

57

*Texas, waiting there [in Parsons] for a lady accompanying
the corpse of her husband. I have a warrant for him. $200 for
his capture, Governor of New Mexico will undoubtedly offer
more, will take train tomorrow for Houston.*
D. Romero, Sheriff of San Miguel County, New Mexico.

A deputy marshal located and arrested Hoodoo the same
day at the Belmont House where he had been staying, waiting
for Mrs. Carson. When she arrived on the noon train, she found
Hoodoo had been arrested and visited him in prison. The *Parsons
Sun* reported, "The meeting between the pair is said to have been
affecting in the extreme, and rather more affectionate than would
be expected under the circumstances." The *Parsons Eclipse* added
that Hoodoo's specific offense in Las Vegas was murder and robbery, and it indicated that seduction and adultery were connected
to the crime.

Soon thereafter, however, Hoodoo hired two local attorneys
and was released when the lawyers managed to prove that the
officers had no legal authority to hold him. "His female companion went south on the M.K. & T. Tuesday noon," the *Parsons Sun*
reported, "he starting several hours ahead on horseback. They will
doubtless meet again further south." Neither he nor the widow
was ever seen again. The *Chicago Times* soon reported that the
justice of the peace, the marshal's widow, and the coffin had been
"skylarking through some of the interior towns of Kansas ever
since. Although Mrs. Carson still clings to her old love, she fol-
lows faithfully in the wanderings of her new mash."

AFTERWORD
Not much is confirmed about Hoodoo's final years. A descendant
of Hyman G. Neill indicated that Hoodoo died in Torreón, Coa-
huila, Mexico, where he left a common-law wife and a son. Two of
Hoodoo's brothers brought back his remains as well as his son to
Lexington, Missouri. Hoodoo was buried there in his family plot
under the name Henry G. Neill.

Years later, records indicated that a woman named Elizabeth Brown was living in Leadville, Colorado. According to reports, she was a heavy drinker, a well-known practitioner of the black arts, and claimed to have been married to a gambler named Hoodoo Brown. She may have been Hoodoo's common-law wife, but this was never proven.

CHAPTER SEVEN

"Mysterious Dave" Mather:
Accused of "Promiscuous Shooting"

*Dave Mather didn't wait for you. If you came to town talkin'
loud about what you intended to do, Dave would find you and
shoot you before you even got started.*

—LOUIS L'AMOUR

"MYSTERIOUS DAVE" MATHER LIVED HIS LIFE SHROUDED IN intrigue and mystery. In his book *Dodge City*, author Tom Clavin says of Mather, "His personality was so taciturn that he made Wyatt Earp seem absolutely giddy." When Mather spoke, which was infrequently, the words were short, to the point. Clavin goes on to say, "There was rarely an expression on his face. The curling of his thin lips was a dramatic outburst."

Definitely a man of mystery, Mather was involved in an incident in Dodge City that puzzled the entire town. Never having spoken much at all, or of spirituality in particular, Mather shocked Bill Tilghman, Bat Masterson's deputy, when "Salvation Sam" came to town. Sam had set up a revival meeting in the Red Dog Saloon with permission from Luke Short, one of the owners. One evening, Tilghman, alone in his office, heard gunfire and immediately ran to where bystanders pointed toward the saloon.

Entering, Tilghman spotted Sam and his followers cowering behind several rows of benches. His gaze traveled over the people and rested on Mather, standing on one side, gun in hand.

Which way would this go? Tilghman opted for calm, not opening fire on Mather. According to Clavin, Tilghman said, "Dave, I need you to give me your gun."

Mather simply stared at him. Tilghman pressed further and promised he wouldn't hurt him. He asked Mather to give him the weapon "so that you don't hurt anybody either." With the patience of someone facing a cornered wild animal, Tilghman slowly approached Mather. After a few moments, Mather handed over the Colt.

No one was injured, but Tilghman asked Sam to swear out a complaint against Mather. The preacher pointed toward the ceiling and said, "Charges against this sinner have been made in Heaven. God will punish him as he sees fit."

Tilghman escorted Mather outside to the boardwalk, where Mather finally spoke. "Hypocrites."

Wondering what exactly was on Mather's mind, the deputy waited. Clavin writes, "In what for him was the equivalent of a Shakespearean soliloquy, Dave continued, 'The preacher asked them to come forward and confess their sins, and after they did the preacher said they could go straight to heaven. I figured to help them take advantage of that opportunity right away, before sinning again and ruining things. But they really didn't want to go, so they're a bunch of hypocrites.'"

Tilghman escorted Mather across the bridge spanning the Arkansas River, suggesting he not come back too soon. Mather got on his horse and rode away—without a word.

Early Years

Born in Saybrook, Connecticut, on August 10, 1851, David Allen Mather was the oldest of three boys. Ulysses Mather, David's father, was a seafaring captain who abandoned his family in 1856

Dave Mather was last seen in 1887. His whereabouts after that were never known.
KANSAS STATE HISTORICAL SOCIETY

and was murdered in Shanghai, China, aboard his ship in 1864. Eyewitnesses recount an angry Chinese cook stabbing Captain Mather. News of his death did not reach Connecticut until two months later, when reports were printed in the Hartford press.

Since he came from a family of lawmen in Massachusetts and rugged English sailors, Mather was proud of his English heritage. He wore royal blue and red often, even as he aged. After their mother's death around 1867, and wanting to follow in their father's footsteps, Mather and his brother Josiah (1854–1932) signed on as crew of a cargo ship bound for New Orleans in 1870. Dave was nineteen, Josiah fifteen. Their youngest brother, George, had died in infancy.

Upon reaching New Orleans, the brothers decided the sea was not where they wanted to spend their time. They headed west, as did many young men. Dave Mather, a smallish man with square but frail shoulders, had dark eyes and a mustache.

"Mysterious Dave" Arrives in Dodge City

Around 1873 in Arkansas, Mather became involved in cattle rustling in Sharp County. His partners? "Dirty Dave" Rudabaugh and Milton J. Yarberry. Mather is named on an 1873 warrant, along with the other two, for the murder and robbery of a prominent rancher. The three fled to Decatur, Texas.

Mather's brother Josiah said that he and Dave had tried to work as buffalo hunters on the Llano Estacado around 1874, but that hadn't lasted long. It's possible that during this time, Mather met Wyatt Earp, Bat Masterson, and Bill Tilghman, who were also following the herds then, as was Hoodoo Brown.

In addition, Mather was often seen around the saloons of Denver, Colorado, always with twin Colts bulging under his coat. He was known to carefully watch the players at the faro, blackjack, and poker tables. By 1874, Mather had arrived in Dodge City, where he nearly died from a knife slash across his stomach during a gambling dispute.

According to historian Howard Bryan, in 1878, Mather and part-time lawman Wyatt Earp were chased out of Mobeetie, in the Texas Panhandle, where they had been peddling phony gold bricks to naïve citizens, claiming the bricks came from a long-lost Spanish gold mine. Mather was also reported to have killed a man in Mobeetie. Various historians deny the Mather–Earp swindle, but just as many agree it is true.

In 1879, Mather hooked up with outlaw "Dutch Henry" Borne, leader of a horse-stealing ring operating from Kansas to eastern Colorado, New Mexico, and the Texas Panhandle. The ring was so big, there were an estimated three hundred members. On one "expedition," Mather was arrested with Borne but was later released. Borne drifted on to Las Vegas, New Mexico, where he became a member of the Dodge City Gang. By that time, it is said, he had become so good at stealing horses that he once sold a sheriff his own recently stolen horse.

Mather's career as a lawman started in 1879. Sheriff Bat Masterson recruited Mather to serve in a posse to enforce the Atchison, Topeka and Santa Fe Railway claims during the Royal Gorge Railroad War. In this posse were J. J. Webb, "Dirty Dave" Rudabaugh, and Doc Holliday. Although the posse was never called to action, Mather had proved unafraid of conflict.

ON TO LAS VEGAS, NEW MEXICO

Mather pushed on, along with other Dodge City characters, and quickly became identified with Hoodoo Brown's Dodge City Gang in Las Vegas, New Mexico. Hoodoo Brown was also the justice of the peace in Las Vegas, and Mather became a member of his merchant police force. Despite Mather's questionable past, he was appointed deputy US marshal.

It's possible he deserved his reputation as a ruthless gang member when, a month later, he became involved in a squabble with a group of soldiers, which turned into a shooting match. The *Las Vegas Gazette* reported on November 22, 1879, that, "Night before last, while the soldiers were stationed in town, several of the boys went to the new town [East Las Vegas] and imbibed a little too much benzine and consequently became noisy and boisterous. They were arrested by the officers of the new town. One of them, however, broke away and started to run. Mr. Matthews [Mather] ordered him to halt, but he refused . . . whereupon he was pursued and fired at some five or six times, one of the shots taking effect in the thumb. Yet the offense committed by the soldiers seems to be rather too small a one to justify such promiscuous shooting. Not only was the life of the offender in danger but also the lives of those on the streets. . . . Officers as well as others should be careful about the use of firearms."

A Legend Was Born

Mather's first real shoot-out was extraordinary, even by Wild West standards. Four cowboys, letting off a lot of steam, rode into town in January 1880, hell-bent on having a good time. According to the *Las Vegas Optic*, the men, well armed, paraded up and down the streets laughing at law officers.

The group's leader, twenty-one-year-old Tom Henry, had reportedly come to the area to steal horses. By January 22, they had disturbed the peace by shooting their guns, boisterous drinking and cursing everyone they met. The four roared into the Close and Patterson Dance Hall on Main Street in East Las Vegas.

Forty-year-old town marshal Joe Carson, Mather's boss, approached the men and asked for their guns—only until they left town. It was a standard practice all over the West. They ignored the lawman, and he repeated the request. According to eyewitnesses, the answer was a barrage of profane insults, which turned into a barrage of bullets. Carson managed to pull his gun from his hip pocket and fire two shots before falling to the floor with nine bullets in his body.

Mather rushed to the scene, jerked out his six-shooter, and opened fire. The dance hall was riddled with at least forty shots. When the considerable smoke cleared, one of the cowboys lay dead and one was down with a bullet through his middle. Marshal Carson was dead.

Wounded, Tom Henry and the only one of his men left uninjured jumped on horses, galloped into the night, and left behind their wounded friend, who was immediately arrested and jailed. News of the shooting spread, and Mather quickly earned the reputation of being quite the man killer, having wounded two and killed one. With the marshal dead, Mather was now acting marshal and immediately appointed Dave Rudabaugh and J. J. Webb as assistant marshals.

A mere three days later, Mather was forced to kill again. On January 25, Mather was summoned to an altercation involving railroad telegrapher Joseph Castello, who, in the heat of an argument with his drunken railroad crew, drew his revolver on them. When Mather arrived, Castello warned him not to approach or he would shoot. The *Las Vegas Optic* reports, "Castello suddenly pointed his murderous weapon at Dave Mather, and with a cocked pistol in his hand, threatened to shoot the officer if he advanced another step. Dave knew his duty and knew the consequences that would result from a delay of action, so he advanced and, in a twinkling of an eye . . . drew his trusty revolver from its place and fired one shot at the determined man, the ball taking effect in Castello's left side below the ribs, penetrating the lung, and ranging downward, through the stomach and liver. Of course the man could not live."

The coroner's jury ruled that Mather's shooting was justifiable and in self-protection. However, Las Vegas had turned too violent for Mather's taste. The final straw was two weeks later when the two escapees from the dance hall shooting were located north of town. Mather sent Webb and others to bring them in, promising their safety behind bars. But he wasn't able to keep that promise as one hundred angry vigilantes broke the two out of jail, along with the injured man, and hanged one at the town's windmill. Before they could hang the other two, Marshal Joe Carson's widow killed them with a shotgun.

LEAVING LAS VEGAS

The public began to suspect that Mather had ties to Hoodoo Brown, the town mob boss, and Mather resigned on March 3, 1880, officially citing low pay as his reason for leaving. However, Mather did not leave East Las Vegas immediately. He was still there as late as March 19, 1880, when he signed his name to a court document intended to help J. J. Webb, who had been charged with murder.

According to various records, Mather spent the next couple of years drifting around Texas and having various minor skirmishes with the law, including a stint in a Texas jail for counterfeiting. It was also reported that in Dallas he became involved with an African American woman who worked as a madam of a brothel called the Long Branch. By 1881, he's reported to have not only

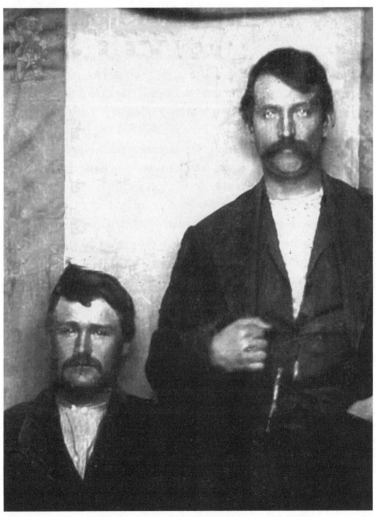

"Mysterious Dave" Mather and Milton Yarberry, unknown location.
AUTHOR'S COLLECTION

left her, but also robbed her, taking two diamond rings and a watch. Seeking revenge, she followed him to Fort Worth, where he worked as a policeman. Wielding a butcher knife, she went after him but was arrested before she got her retribution.

RETURN TO DODGE CITY

Next, Mather drifted to El Paso, Texas, where he served briefly as assistant marshal. After an altercation in a brothel in which Mather was slightly wounded, he rode back to Dodge City.

While Mather had been away from Dodge City, the Santa Fe Railroad had pressured town leaders to clean up "their" town. The railroad was big business, and they made the rules. The existence of open gambling, drinking, prostitution, and dance halls had heated up as a major town issue. Those who liked Dodge City the way it was, known as the Resistance, and those who wanted it refined were still at odds when Mather arrived. On June 1, 1883, he was hired as assistant city marshal. Soon afterward, he became co-owner of the Opera House Saloon on Front Street.

Operating the Opera House wasn't as easy, or as profitable, as he'd imagined. Much to his chagrin, the city passed Ordinance No. 83, which outlawed dance halls within city limits. This law was enforced against his Opera House Saloon, preventing it from operating as a dance hall, the city council citing its prominent downtown location. However, the council took no action against Tom Nixon's Lady Gay Saloon, which also featured dancing, supposedly due to its remote location, and possibly due to Nixon's friendship with the mayor. For several months, Nixon and Mather battled to put each other out of business.

THE BEER WAR

In retaliation, Mather began a price war on beer. He charged only five cents a glass—half the price of his competitors. Nixon and the other Dodge City saloon owners pressured the beer wholesalers to cut off Mather's supply. Mather at long last backed down.

Adding insult to injury, in 1884, the city government replaced Mather with Nixon as assistant marshal, and the brewing feud erupted. On the evening of July 18, 1884, Nixon drew a gun and fired at Mather, but he ended up hitting a post and spraying Mather with splinters. Mather had powder burns on his cheek. Nixon posted bond on charges of attempted murder. The *Dodge City Democrat* published an article on the shooting, saying the situation was "by all appearances not yet at an end."

Three days later, Mather walked down a staircase and fired four bullets into Nixon, killing him instantly. Later, Mather was heard to say, "I ought to have killed him six months ago." Despite supporting testimony from Bat Masterson and Dodge City sheriff Patrick Shugrue, Mather's case was sent to trial. His attorney obtained a change of venue to Kinsley, Kansas, and the trial began on December 29, 1884. It lasted only three days, and the jury deliberated a total of seven minutes before declaring Mather not guilty. The *Kinsley Mercury* wrote, "The verdict was a proper one, as the weight of the testimony showed that Nixon was the aggressor in the affray and that Mather was justified in the shooting." The *Dodge City Times* noted, "The reading of the verdict, by the court, was interrupted by demonstrations of approval from the audience."

Months later, Mather was joined by his brother Josiah. Both were charged with murder as a result of a gun battle at the Junction Saloon on May 10, 1885. Witnesses said that Mather and David Barnes, who sold groceries out of his house, had been playing cards when an argument erupted over money. Mather shot Barnes, who was armed. A bullet went through Mather's hat, grazing his forehead. An estimated dozen shots were fired in the following ten seconds. Josiah shot from behind the bar. When the smoke cleared, Barnes was dead and two bystanders were wounded. The Mather brothers were released on three thousand dollars bond but never showed up for their trial. Both had disappeared.

Afterword: The Mystery Continues

What happened to "Mysterious Dave" Mather? Hard to tell, exactly. One newspaper in 1885 reported Mather being a deputy marshal in New Kiowa, Kansas, where he remained for a year. Mather had moved there with his friend "Black Dave" and opened a saloon. "Black Dave" soon killed a soldier in a brawl, and Mather raised money for his defense. When some of the dead soldier's friends threatened to come and lynch Mather just for being Black's partner, Mather took the money he had raised and left town.

Two years later it was said he was living alone in a cabin near Long Pine, Nebraska. He left there in 1888, telling friends he was heading south for a warmer climate. Again, he vanished.

But the story doesn't end there. Tales of this famous man of mystery continued for years. One story had him traveling to San Francisco and taking a ship to Vancouver, Canada. Another had him being left for dead on railroad tracks in Dallas, Texas, in 1886. Others say he traveled to the Northwest Territories, where he enlisted with the Royal Canadian Mounted Police (RCMP) but looted the stage he was sent to guard and escaped with £20,000. In 1922, the RCMP refuted the claim he had ever joined them. Brother Josiah reported that Mather was killed by moonshiners in the mountains of Tennessee. But what is true is that Josiah never saw or heard from his brother again after they parted in Dodge City.

The truth about "Mysterious Dave" Mather continues to remain a mystery.

CHAPTER EIGHT

The Dalton Brothers: They Wanted to "Best" the James Gang

Best anything Jesse James ever did—rob two banks at once, in broad daylight.

—Bob Dalton

THE DALTON BROTHERS CAME FROM A FAMILY OF FIFTEEN SIB-lings, most born in Missouri before the family migrated to Indian Territory (present-day Oklahoma) in 1882. James Lewis Dalton and Adeline Younger, the aunt of the equally famous Younger Gang, produced: Louis Kossuth, Charles Benjamin "Ben," Henry Coleman "Cole," Littleton Lee "Lit," Frank, Gratton "Grat," William Marion "Bill," Eva, Robert Reddick "Bob," Emmett, Bea Elizabeth, Leona Randolph, Mason Fracks "Bill," Nancy "Nanny," and Simon "Sam." One of the siblings did not live through infancy. Of all those, only three comprised the infamous Dalton Gang—Bob, Emmett, and Grat. Their father, James, was a horse trader and saloon operator in the 1840s and 1850s when he married their mother, Adeline. Adeline's brother was the father of Bob, Cole, and James Younger.

Frank Dalton (1859–1887)

Described as one of the bravest and most efficient officers on the marshal's force, Frank was always an upstanding citizen. In 1882 he was commissioned as a US deputy marshal at Fort Smith, Arkansas, at age twenty-three. Although he was not paid well—no lawman was—he insisted on sending his paychecks home to his extensive family. The territory was wild, lawmen being few and far between. Constantly in the saddle hunting outlaws, he realized he needed more men. He enlisted the help of his brothers Bob and Grat, swearing them in as US deputy marshals and having them accompany him in posses.

On November 27, 1887, Frank and another deputy, Jim Cole, rode across the Arkansas River from Fort Smith into Indian Territory to arrest three whiskey bootleggers who were also charged with stealing horses. Figuring the men would not put up much of a fight, Frank was surprised they attacked as he approached their camp. One man fled into the woods, but the other two took up arms and shot. The first bullet hit Frank square in the chest, knocking him back and to the ground. However, he continued to shoot until his gun jammed.

Frank's deputy reacted, returning fire and hitting two of the bootleggers. Believing Frank to be dead, the deputy rushed back to Fort Smith for assistance. However, unknown to the deputy, Frank was still alive when he left. But soon, a noted murderer and horse thief who was in the area happened upon Frank, recognized him, and shot him again.

When the deputy returned with other lawmen, Frank was dead, as were two of the bootleggers. The man who killed Frank was soon located and killed. Frank was twenty-eight when he died and was buried in the Elmwood Cemetery in Coffeyville, Kansas. Today, he is remembered by the US Marshals Service on their Roll Call of Honor.

THEY TRIED TO GO STRAIGHT

Frank's death lay heavily on the family. In his memory, the Dalton brothers served with distinction on the law's side for many months. But lawmen's pay, being notoriously low and at times nonexistent, prompted the men to take up other, more lucrative, occupations.

BOB DALTON (1868–1892)

Robert "Bob" Reddick Dalton killed his first man when he was nineteen. Being a deputy marshal, Bob claimed it was self-defense. Others disagreed, saying there had been hard feelings between the two—over a woman.

Following the incident, Bob requested reassignment and was commissioned in the Western District at Fort Smith as a US deputy marshal and was assigned to work for the Wichita, Kansas, court. During this time, he also served as chief of police for the Osage Indian Nation. In August 1889, Bob was sent to Coffeyville, Kansas, to arrest a man charged with stealing horses and peddling whiskey in Indian Territory.

When Bob approached, the man drew his gun. Bob shot, killing the man. When he brought the body back to Fort Smith, expecting the usual reward money, he discovered there was no reward offered. Bob received nothing for his efforts. In addition, when no one claimed the outlaw's body, as was the custom of the day, Bob had to foot the burial expenses.

Bob began to drink heavily and became restless. He was given the job of organizing a police force in the Osage Nation, and he took Emmett along as a deputy. Grat, meanwhile, stayed at Fort Smith. Emmett and Bob maintained their good reputations in the Osage Nation until July 1890, when they began stealing horses from the reservation as well as outlying areas. Eventually stockmen organized to capture them, forcing Bob and Emmett to flee. Hiding out in caves along the bluffs on the Canadian River about seventy miles southwest of Kingfisher, Oklahoma, they sent for Grat to help.

Grat tried to get them food, horses, and ammunition but was arrested and thrown in jail at Fort Smith—a jail where, as a deputy, he had placed prisoners himself. After two weeks, Grat was released in the hope he would lead the law to his brothers. Bob and Emmett, however, had already taken a train west.

FORMING THE DALTON GANG

Along the way, Emmett, who had worked as a cowboy on the Bar X Bar Ranch in Oklahoma, met up with George "Bitter Creek" Newcomb, Bill McElhanie, and "Blackfaced Charlie" Bryant. Bob recruited them all to join his gang.

They rode into the mining town of Silver City, New Mexico Territory, where they committed their first robbery. The men enjoyed the saloons, the bawdy houses, and the excitement a new mining camp brought. They sat in on a faro game in what Emmett later recalled was a Mexican casino, where they lost heavily. In a 1996 *True West* article, J. R. Sanders wrote, "An Easterner observed in 1872 that 'there is rarely a word spoken during the progress of a deal, for faro is the most quiet, and in that respect, the most gentlemanly of all games.' But this same writer also warned that 'faro honestly played is a game of pure chance, and sometimes favors the unfortunate who meddles with it.' Players liked the seemingly favorable odds." In an honest game, chances were 50/50 to win. More often, the dealer won.

Convinced the game was crooked, the brothers pulled guns and took back what they had lost. And a few extra dollars ended up in their pockets as well. Bob and Emmett fled to California, where their brother Mason, who went by the name Bill (not to be confused with William Marion Dalton, who also went by Bill), was a successful farmer and rancher. Before arriving there, Bob and Emmett relieved the Southern Pacific Railroad of sixty thousand dollars.

After relocating to Oklahoma to be closer to the family farm, between May 1891 and July 1892, the Dalton brothers robbed four trains in the Indian Territory. One at Adair, Oklahoma, near the Arkansas border, produced meager results. The men then went through the train station and took what they could find in the express and baggage rooms. Still not satisfied with their haul, they decided to wait for the next train.

They sat on a bench on the platform, talking and smoking, Winchester rifles across their knees. The train arrived at 9:45 p.m. All eight armed guards on the train happened to be in the end car when it pulled up to the station. The brothers backed a wagon up to the express car and unloaded all the contents. When the guards realized what was happening, they fired at the gang through the car windows and from behind the train. In that exchange, two hundred shots were fired; none of the Dalton gang was hit. Two men, sitting on the porch of the drugstore near the depot, were hit several times by stray shots. One was killed. The Dalton Gang fled and disappeared, likely hiding out in one of several caves near Tulsa or at their sister Bea's house in Meade, Kansas. A tunnel ran ninety-five feet from a pantry in the kitchen area to the barn, making a terrific hiding place and getaway channel. Reportedly, the tunnel was used frequently.

GRATTON DALTON (1865–1892)

Grat was hired into Frank's job as US deputy marshal after he was killed in 1887. The next year, Grat took a bullet in his left arm when he was trying to serve an arrest warrant on an Indian outlaw. By August 1889, he was working as a deputy marshal for the Muskogee court in Indian Territory. The following year, he assisted in arresting a number of fugitives, but when he forced a young black boy to place an apple on his head then shot off the fruit, the marshal found out and dismissed Grat for misuse of authority. Undaunted, he then worked as a posse man for other deputy marshals in the area. In September 1890, Grat was arrested for stealing horses but was later released due to lack of evidence.

Deciding Indian Territory was not the best place for him, Grat joined his brothers in California, where they robbed more trains. In 1891, accused of a train robbery that witnesses said he did not commit, he was taken into custody anyway. A long stretch at San Quentin or Folsom Prison was in his future. Somehow, he managed to break out of the county jail and made his escape. Now realizing California wasn't a good place to be, he galloped back to Oklahoma and waited for his brothers to return.

EMMETT DALTON (1871–1937)
Unlike his brothers, Emmett was never appointed US deputy marshal, but he did serve with them on posses.

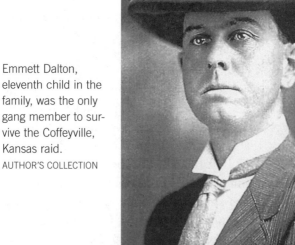

Emmett Dalton, eleventh child in the family, was the only gang member to survive the Coffeyville, Kansas raid.
AUTHOR'S COLLECTION

ONE FINAL ROBBERY: THE DALTON GANG RAIDS COFFEYVILLE, KANSAS

On October 5, 1892, the sun radiated warmth and good cheer over Coffeyville, Kansas. Timing their arrival for the moment the banks opened, the Dalton Gang rode into town, focused on robbing two banks—concurrently. Figuring they were known around Coffeyville since the family lived near there, they thought they should disguise themselves. The gang of five donned false beards. They entered from the west at 8 a.m., hoping no one would recognize them. But the townspeople did.

In his mind, and out loud on occasion, Bob had boasted he could best Jesse James. Heck, he'd said, he could rob two banks at once. This play was most appealing since it would be their last robbery, their swan song, so to speak. The plan? Rob the Condon Bank and First National. Take the money, gallop down to Mexico, and enjoy life. By now, nearly every lawman and railroad detective was hunting the Daltons, so getting out of the country would be a good idea.

Approaching the downtown area, they turned west into an alley (known today as Death Alley) and tied their horses at the end. With rifles and guns in hand, the three Daltons—Emmett, Grat, and Bob—stepped into the plaza. Grat, along with Dick Broadwell and Bill Power, entered the Condon Bank and demanded money. The bank manager calmly told them that the lock was on a timer and wouldn't open for several more minutes. Bamboozled, Grat and his men stood waiting instead of trying the door. In reality? The safe had no timer, but it did contain forty thousand dollars.

A passerby glanced in the bank's window, recognized Emmett Dalton, realized a robbery was in progress, and quietly ran across the street to a hardware store. Townspeople were not armed—not even the sheriff—so they grabbed rifles and pistols from Isham's Hardware, which still stands at its original location. With loaded weapons, they took positions behind wagons, barrels, and hay bales.

While the citizens were positioning themselves, Emmett and Bob successfully managed to hold up the First National Bank located across the street from the Condon Bank. When they stepped outside, the shooting started. Darting back inside, they rushed out through the back door. As they came around the building's corner, Bob shot a man in the heart. Still on their feet, the two ran north from the bank and west down the street toward their horses, nearly two blocks away. During that run, Bob shot two more citizens.

Hearing the commotion outside, Grat and his two partners decided to make a run for their horses without the money. As they exited the Condon Bank, the marshal stepped into the alley, looked back over his shoulder, and was shot by Grat. Men fired on the gang from all directions. Grat lay bleeding in the alley; Dick Broadwell had been shot several times before dying. Bill Power, wounded, made it to his horse and headed west. He fell dead on the edge of town. Bob continued to fire even though he'd been shot several times. Emmett received twenty-three gunshot wounds (through his right arm, below his shoulder, through his hip and groin, and between eighteen and thirty buckshots in his back) and survived. He made it to his horse and started for freedom, but he noticed Bob was still alive. He circled back, offering his hand to his brother. At that point, he was hit with a double-barreled blast and fell to the ground.

The gunfight lasted less than ten minutes, but eight men died—four from the Gang and four defending the town. Bob and Grat were buried in the back portion of the Elmwood Cemetery in Coffeyville.

On October 6, 1892, the *Galveston Daily News* reported, "The Dalton Gang has been exterminated—wiped off the face of the earth." But not all died. Recovering, Emmett stood trial in Independence, Kansas, pleading guilty to murder. He was sentenced to life in prison at Kansas State Penitentiary in Lansing. After fourteen and a half years, the governor of Kansas pardoned him in

1907. In 1908, he married Julia Lewis in Bartlesville, Oklahoma, before settling in Tulsa, where he was a police officer for a time. They eventually moved to California, where Emmett worked as a building contractor. Later, he wrote a book about the Dalton

Grat Dalton served as US Deputy Marshal at Ft. Smith, Arkansas.
AUTHOR'S COLLECTION

Gang exploits—*When the Daltons Rode*, published in 1931. He died in 1937 and is buried in Oklahoma.

AFTERWORD

Obsessed with making a name for himself more prominent than his brothers', William Marion "Bill" Dalton partnered with Dalton Gang member Bill Doolin. A couple of weeks after the Coffeyville Raid, they sent a letter to the sheriff and newspaper in Coffeyville. In it, they warned that not everyone in the Dalton Gang was dead, and the remainder were planning to sweep back into town and not only rob both banks, but also deliver hell and damnation to the entire town. Naturally, citizens were nervous. They came into town from outlying areas to help protect property and lives.

Two weeks after the Coffeyville fiasco, Bill Dalton and Bill Doolin robbed the Ford County Bank eighteen miles *west* of Cof-

Condon Bank, one of the two banks in Coffeyville targeted by the Dalton Gang.
KANSAS STATE HISTORICAL SOCIETY

Condon Bank after the holdup. Can you find three bullet holes?
KANSAS STATE HISTORICAL SOCIETY

feyville, in Spearville, Kansas, getting away with all the cash on hand and $1,500 in treasury notes. They never did rob Coffeyville.

The Bills did not get along. Friction mounted between the two. Each claimed to be the leader of the recently formed gang. Bill Doolin, more educated and probably more intelligent than Dalton, continued to plot and plan further bank heists and train robberies. Eventually, the two Bills went separate ways.

On May 23, 1894, Bill Dalton and his new gang robbed the First National Bank at Longview, Texas. This was the gang's only job. On June 8, 1894, a posse approached Dalton's home near Ardmore, Oklahoma. Resisting arrest, Dalton reportedly jumped through a window and ran toward the posse, ignoring warnings. He was killed immediately.

The famous Dalton Gang may be gone, but they are definitely not forgotten.

CHAPTER NINE

Tom Horn:
Hanged by "Julian Gallows"

I saw him ride by. He didn't stop, but went straight on up the creek in plain sight of everyone. All he wanted was to be seen, as his reputation was so great that his presence in a community had the desired effect. Within a week three settlers in the neighborhood sold their holdings and moved out. That was the end of cattle rustling on the North Laramie.

— FERGIE MITCHELL, RANCHER
ON THE NORTH LARAMIE RIVER

THE WYOMING MORNING WAS COOL, TYPICAL FOR MID-JULY, BUT foggy. Temperatures hovered in the low 40s shortly before sunrise when Tom Horn sighted his rifle on a fourteen-year-old boy.

KILLING THE KID

Just as the sun rose, Willie Nickell, wearing an oversized coat and slump hat like his father's, drove a wagon to the gate of the family homestead forty miles northwest of Cheyenne, dismounted, and opened the gate. Shot in the back, the teenager staggered to his feet, took another bullet, and fell dead.

Tom Horn spent most of his time in jail plaiting rope.
AUTHOR'S COLLECTION

Charged with tracking down and "dealing justice" to those suspected of stealing cattle or encroaching on their range, area cattlemen had hired Tom Horn as a range detective against the growing number of rustlers and sheepherders roaming the area. Horn had visited the cattle-ranching family of Jim and Dora Miller near Iron Mountain, Wyoming, on July 15, 1901. Miller and his neighbor, Kels Nickell, had already had several disputes following Nickell's introduction of sheep into the area. Miller frequently accused Nickell of allowing his sheep to graze on his cattle ranch.

Horn's sense of justice was delivered by a .30-.30 Winchester.

ROUGH CHILDHOOD: A BOY AND HIS DOG

Thomas Horn Jr., "Tom," was born November 21, 1860, to Thomas S. Horn Sr. and Mary Ann Mariche on their family farm in rural northeastern Scotland County, Missouri. In his autobiography, *Life of Tom Horn: Government Scout & Interpreter*, Horn devoted a chapter to his childhood and told of his family's fundamentalist religion, his father a Campbellite (Disciples of Christ) who would, according to Horn, resort to beatings to enforce discipline. The "regular thumpings" delivered by his father and occasional whippings by his mother may have influenced his willingness to take a life.

Horn's family was of German descent and bilingual. As the fourth and youngest child, he had one brother and two sisters. His father had moved from Ohio in the 1840s and was known to be an industrious, capable farmer and trader who kept his family's affairs private. It has been implied that the elder Tom made unfavorable comparisons between Tom Jr. and his siblings, and that he thought young Tom never quite measured up.

Horn reportedly showed an aptitude for hunting and marksmanship at an early age.

His mother would send him out hunting "varmints" that raided the farm, and he always took along Shedrick (known as Shed), his trusty sidekick dog.

He wrote that farm work left him short of time for things that were more important—fishing, tracking, hunting, and raiding bees' nests in the company of Shed, his only friend and companion. In 1874, the dog was senselessly killed when young Tom got into a fight with two migrant farm boys who beat him and killed Shed with a shotgun. In his writings, Horn describes Shed as "the sharer of my joys and sorrows. . . . There never was a better dog! . . . That [the killing of Shed] was the first and only real sorrow of my life." After the shooting, he carried the big dog (known to be large enough to pull Horn's father in a cart) back to the farm and buried him.

Shortly after his dog was killed, Horn fought his father. The older man prevailed, but young Tom told him that this "thumping" would be the last one because he was going to leave home. The beating was so severe that Horn had to lie in the barn all night. In his autobiography he states that after a week, when he was well enough to leave, he kissed his mother for the last time, looked at Shed's grave, and headed west. He was fourteen.

A different version of Horn's leaving-home story says that his father threw him out of the house, turning him over to Mexican teamsters on the Santa Fe Trail. Yet another version, according to a 2014 *True West* article by Larry Ball, an Arkansas State University professor emeritus, states that "he was probably several years older when he left, and he maintained contact with his family."

Whichever story is true, Horn drifted for years, working on the railroad, driving freight wagons and stagecoaches, and then signing on as a scout for the US Army.

In his autobiography, writing of the period after he left home, Horn describes his employment with the railroad in Kansas, during which time he earned twenty-one dollars for twenty-six days' work. He writes of a job as a driver for the Overland Mail in Santa Fe for fifty dollars a month and "use of a rifle."

YEARS IN ARIZONA

Eventually, Horn drifted to Arizona where he became a wrangler for seventy-five dollars a month. He outfitted himself with a good horse, tack, and a rifle. US Army quartermaster records indicate Horn was employed in September 1881 as a teamster at Whipple Barracks, near Prescott. He soon moved to the pack train service and remained there until 1885, when he became a scout, working with another scout, Mickey Free, who had been the catalyst for the George Bascom Affair at Apache Pass in 1860.

In 1860, freshly minted 2nd Lt. George Bascom from Arizona's Ft. Buchanan was charged with rescuing twelve-year-old Felix Telles (who later became Mickey Free), who'd been kidnapped from his ranch by Indians. Bascom accused Cochise, whose tribe was innocent. A series of violent retaliatory actions from both the Apache and the US Army resulted in a declaration of war between the two factions. Bascom's actions put Apache/US relations back forty years.

By November 1885, Horn had earned the position of chief of scouts at Fort Bowie, Arizona. During one operation, a Mexican militia attacked Horn's camp, and he was wounded in his arm.

Being an excellent tracker from an early age paid off for Horn. In 1886, he tracked Geronimo and his tribe to their hideout in the Sierra Gordo area near Sonora, Mexico. Horn rode into their camp to negotiate the Apache's surrender, thus ending the last great Indian war in America. Horn personally escorted Geronimo to the train at Bowie Station that transported the captives into exile in Florida.

One important person left out of Horn's autobiography was his common-law wife when he lived on Arizona's San Carlos Reservation. Sawn, whom he called "housekeeper," may well have been his wife. In the Apache language, *Sawn* means "my wife" or "my old lady." She also may have birthed one or two of his children.

Horn showed his flair for cowboying when he won the world championship in steer roping at the Globe, Arizona, Fourth of

July Celebration in 1889 with a record-setting time of fifty-eight seconds. Horn then traveled to the territorial fair held near Phoenix (population three thousand), the new territorial capital of Arizona. Competing again in steer roping, he won.

After leaving the army, Horn built his own ranch in Aravaipa Canyon, Arizona. His ranch consisted of a hundred head of cattle and twenty-six horses, and he also laid claim in the Deer Creek Mining District near the canyon. Unfortunately, cattle thieves stormed his ranch one night and stole all his stock, leaving him a tremendous loss and bankruptcy. This incident would mark Horn's hatred and disdain for thieves, which probably led to his entering the profession of range detective.

Pleasant Valley War

Horn worked on an Arizona ranch, where he claimed that he was the "mediator" of the Pleasant Valley conflict throughout the war, serving as a deputy sheriff under three famous Arizona lawmen. One was a close personal friend of Horn and mayor of Prescott, Arizona, William Owen "Buckey" O'Neill, who became captain of the Prescott Grays in 1886, the local unit of the Arizona Militia. According to an article in *Arizona Military History* by Chaplain Thomas E. Troxell, on February 5, 1886, a convicted murderer was hanged. O'Neill and the Prescott Grays stood honor guard for the event. When the trap dropped, O'Neill fainted, which caused him severe embarrassment. He later wrote a story called "The Horse of the Hash-Knife Brand." In it, a member of a posse admits to nearly fainting at the hanging of a horse thief.

Horn was deputy sheriff under Commodore Perry Owens and Glenn Reynolds during the Pleasant Valley War, tracking rustlers and bringing in men who had arrest warrants on their heads. Horn also participated in the lynching of three suspected rustlers in August 1888. During this time, he developed an interest in law enforcement. Serving well as a deputy sheriff, Horn drew the attention of the Pinkerton National Detective Agency for his tracking abilities. In 1890, he reportedly left his Apache family to join the Pinkertons.

As a Pinkerton

In 1891, Horn joined the Pinkerton Detective Agency, which hired him to track down and apprehend—violently if necessary—Western outlaws who were preying on Pinkerton clients. The clients were banks and railroads that could afford to pay for private law enforcement where the public system failed them. Some reports claim he was estranged from his Missouri family, but when he became a Pinkerton operative in Denver, Colorado, his sister Maude served as his housekeeper.

Characterized as fearless, Horn proved it on several occasions. He was over two hundred pounds and six feet two inches tall at a time when the average man weighed perhaps one hundred sixty and stood five foot six. One day he rode alone into the famous Hole-in-the-Wall outlaw stronghold and called out Peg-Leg Watson, wanted for a recent train robbery. Watson emerged from a cabin with a pistol in each hand. Horn, Winchester held loosely at his side, walked steadily toward him across an open field. Awed by his bravery—or stupidity—Watson never fired a shot. Horn took him to jail without a struggle, and the incident helped make Horn a living legend in the West.

By the mid-1890s, the cattle business in Wyoming and Colorado was changing due to the arrival of homesteaders and new ranchers. The homesteaders, referred to as "nesters" or "grangers" by the big operators, had moved into the territory in large numbers. By doing so, they decreased the availability of water for the herds of the larger cattle barons.

During the Johnson County War, Horn worked for the Wyoming Stock Growers Association as well as for the Pinkertons, who had assigned him to work undercover in the county. He is alleged to have been involved in the killing of two men on April

9, 1892, and was a prime suspect for the assassinations of two ranchers. The Pinkerton Agency forced him to resign in 1894.

In his memoir, *Two Evil Isms: Pinkertonism and Anarchism,* Pinkerton detective Charlie Siringo wrote: "William A. Pinkerton told me that Tom Horn was guilty of the crime, but that his people could not allow him to go to prison while in their employ." Siringo would later indicate that he respected Horn's abilities at tracking and that he was a very talented agent, but that he had a wicked element.

AS A WYOMING RANGE DETECTIVE

For several years the big Wyoming cattlemen had been fighting a vigilante war in Johnson County against a diverse group of small farmers, sheep ranchers, and rustlers. By 1894, negative publicity had made a public war too costly. Instead, the ranchers shifted to more stealthy means, hiring Horn as a range detective for his gun-handling skills. He could shoot from two hundred yards—accurately and deadly.

JOINING THE ARMY AS A PACKER

Horn continued to serve as a range detective, but when the Spanish-American War in Cuba began in 1898, he signed up as a packer for the Fifth Corps. He left Tampa for Cuba, where he was in charge of Teddy Roosevelt's pack mule and horse trains. He personally witnessed the assault on San Juan Hill. Although the packers were civilian noncombatants, they were still prone to attacks by Cuban rebels. Horn recalled that he and his men were under constant fire as they delivered rations and ammunition to the soldiers.

No one in his group of packers was ever wounded, but many contracted yellow fever, including Horn. At one point he was bedridden and deemed unfit for combat. Upon recovering, he returned to Wyoming, working again as a rustler hunter, this time for wealthy cattle baron John C. Coble in 1901. Coble belonged to the Wyoming Stock Men's Association.

THE SHOOTING

Disputes between the cattle growers and sheep growers were frequent and violent. Horn spent time at the ranch of Jim Miller, a cattle grower at the center of the Range Wars. There, he met Glendolene M. Kimmell, a young teacher at the Iron Mountain School. Both the large Miller family and the Kels Nickell family supported Ms. Kimmell, and as was the custom, she boarded with the Millers. Horn entertained her with accounts of his adventures. One day Horn and menfolk of the Miller family went fishing; he and Victor Miller, a son about Horn's age of forty-one, also practiced shooting, both of them with .30-.30s.

The Miller and Nickell families were the only ones to have children at the school. Ms. Kimmell had been advised of the families' ongoing feud and found it often played out by the children during recess. On July 18, 1901, Willie Nickell, the fourteen-year-old son of sheep ranchers Kels and Mary Nickell, was found murdered near their homestead gate. A coroner's inquest investigated the murder.

On August 4, 1901, Kels Nickell, Willie's father, was shot and wounded. In addition, between sixty and eighty of his sheep were found shot or clubbed to death. Two of the younger Nickell children later reported seeing two men leaving on horses, a bay and a gray, like those owned by Jim Miller. On August 6, Deputy Sheriff Peter Warlaumont and Deputy US Marshal Joe LeFors came to Iron Mountain and arrested Jim Miller and his sons Victor and Gus on suspicion of shooting Kels Nickell. They were jailed on August 7 and released the following day on bond.

The fact that teenager Willie Nickell was killed with a long-range rifle naturally turned heads toward Tom Horn. His reputation as a violent man-killer was earned, and it was well known that he carried a Winchester and could shoot accurately from two hundred yards. No one was arrested right away, although speculation abounded as to who did it.

THE "CONFESSION"

The killing was immediately attributed to Horn but couldn't be proven. Legendary lawman Joe LeFors, a renowned tracker, resolved to bring Horn to justice. LeFors rode to Denver, got Horn drunk in a small saloon, and had deputies hidden where they could write down anything he said. Although Horn did not directly admit to the killing, he did describe it in such detail that LeFors arrested him for it.

During his subsequent trial back in Cheyenne, Horn's own words were sufficient to result in a guilty verdict and a death sentence. Horn allegedly said young Willie Nickell was shot from about three hundred yards, and then he boldly remarked, "It was the best shot that I ever made and the dirtiest trick I ever done. I thought at one time he would get away."

This 1890 Remington was given to Horn by John Coble in service to Swan Cattle Company.
GUNSINTERNATIONAL.COM

COLD-BLOODED KILLER OR JUST A DARN GOOD MARKSMAN? THE TRIAL

Horn's trial went to jury on October 23, 1903, and the next day returned a guilty verdict. He was sentenced to hang. His attorneys filed a petition with the Wyoming Supreme Court for a new trial. While in jail, Horn wrote his autobiography, published posthumously in 1904, mostly giving an account of his early life. It contained little about the case.

The court denied a new trial. Convinced of Horn's innocence, schoolteacher Glendolene Kimmell sent an affidavit to the governor with testimony reportedly saying that Victor Miller was guilty of Nickell's murder. The governor chose not to intervene in the case.

HANGED BY THE JULIAN GALLOWS

Horn was executed with a new, and supposedly more humane, method of hanging that relied on the emptying of a bucket of water to trigger the release of the trap door upon which the condemned man was standing: "Instantly the sibilant sound of running water permeated the breathless stillness; the instrument of death had begun to operate. To the straining ears of the listeners that little sound had the magnitude of that of a rushing torrent." The original report was written by reporter Charles Thompson and was first published in the Denver, Colorado, *Posse of Westerners*.

Horn was one of the few people to have been hanged by water-powered gallows, the "Julian Gallows." James P. Julian, a Cheyenne, Wyoming, architect, designed the contraption in 1892. The trap door was connected to a lever, which pulled the plug out of a barrel of water. This would cause a lever with a counterweight to rise, pulling on the support beam under the gallows. When enough pressure was applied, the beam broke free, opening the trap and hanging the condemned man. The idea was that no man was the official executioner.

Horn was buried in the Columbia Cemetery in Boulder, Colorado, on December 3, 1903. Rancher and friend Jim Coble paid for his coffin and a stone to mark his grave.

THE DEBATE

Did Tom Horn actually kill the teenager? If so, was it intentional or accidental? One side asks: Who can trust a drunken confession? Convict someone solely on the basis of that confession? They claim a number of reliable witnesses testified that Horn was at least twenty miles away at the time. Even the old Apache warrior Geronimo expressed his doubts about Horn's charges, saying he "did not believe [Horn] guilty."

The other side says Horn killed the boy even though he identified him as a teenager, not the older Nickell. Historian Chip Carlson believed the prosecution made no effort to investigate other possible suspects, including Victor Miller. According to Carlson, "Willie Nickell was not wearing his father's clothes or hat, as has been mentioned earlier. Joe LeFors said that when he visited the Nickell home he saw Willie's bloody clothes. Willie's mother also stated in testimony that he was wearing his own clothes."

In essence, Horn's reputation and history made him an easy target for the prosecution, as did his propensity for embellishing stories—for "bragging" a bit. No, bragging *a lot*.

Yet Ms. Kimmel, the schoolteacher with whom Horn had been linked in legend and lore, perceived that he was an anachronism. Kimmell wrote in the appendix to Horn's autobiography, "Riding hard, drinking hard, fighting hard, so passed his days until he was crushed between the grindstones of two civilizations. Substitute 'centuries' for 'civilizations.'"

CHAPTER TEN

Henry Newton Brown:
He Rode with Billy the Kid

*It is said that he is one of the quickest men on the trigger in
the Southwest.*
            —CALDWELL (KANSAS) POST, 1883

HENRY NEWTON BROWN PROBABLY DIDN'T KNOW WHAT HE WAS
signing up for when he chose to ride with Billy Bonney and his
pals in 1878. He didn't know what was ahead when he agreed
to be a "Regulator" in the Lincoln County feud between James
Dolan, who partnered with rancher L. G. Murphy, and English
businessman John Tunstall, who partnered with lawyer Alexander McSween. Brown was accused, along with Bonney and John
Middleton, of killing Sheriff William Brady, although Bonney
was the only one who went to trial. And Brown certainly didn't
know he would become a major player in the most famous and
well-researched, well-documented, well-argued, climactic gunfight in history—the Five Day War, the climax of the Lincoln
County War.

Early Life

Orphaned at a young age, Henry Newton Brown, born in 1857, and his sister were reared on their uncle's farm in Phelps County, ten miles south of Rolla, Missouri. There he lived with his Uncle Jasper and Aunt Aldamira. At seventeen, he left home and headed west.

A Lincoln County War Regulator: Rode with Billy the Kid

For a time Brown worked on a ranch in eastern Colorado, then spent a season hunting buffalo in Texas. In 1876 he killed a man in the Texas Panhandle, then gravitated south to turbulent Lincoln County, New Mexico. Brown signed on as a cowpuncher and rustler with Major L. G. Murphy at his ranch thirty miles west of Lincoln, working there for eighteen months. Brown quit in a rather heated argument, presumably over wages.

Brown changed allegiances and went to work for Murphy's nemesis, rancher John Chisolm (not to be confused with Jesse Chisum of the famous Chisolm Trail), who was in partnership with John Tunstall and Alexander McSween on Tunstall's Rio Feliz Ranch. Brown worked alongside Billy the Kid and other cowboys who officially formed a gang, calling themselves "The Regulators," or as some refer to them, Tunstall's private army.

Blue-eyed with sandy hair, a mustache, and a slim, wiry build, Brown was nineteen, a year older than Billy, when they met. Having already shot a man, Brown knew how to use guns, and, some people thought, resorted to them too readily. "Nervy," judged former Regulator Frank Coe in a deposition on February 20, 1928, "but not smart like Kid."

Brown was smart enough to realize he and the other Regulators had been hired as much for their shooting skills as for their mastery of cowpunching. They spent some time at the ranch on the Rio Feliz, where the only building, a crude two-room adobe,

Henry Newton Brown joined Billy the Kid as a "Regulator" during the Lincoln County War.
AUTHOR'S COLLECTION

afforded inadequate shelter and few comforts. The men would ride to Lincoln on chores and do whatever Tunstall needed.

Blazer's Mill, Lincoln, New Mexico

In February 1878, a war erupted in Lincoln County, and the Lawrence Murphy–James Dolan group hired Bob Olinger, a known gun hand. Olinger was among the riders who caught John Tunstall in a lonely ravine near Pajarito Spring and murdered him in cold blood. Although several riders participated in the murder, only James Dolan and one other were charged with being accessories to murder. Billy took Tunstall's death hard and vowed revenge. On April 1, 1878, Brown, Billy, and others ambushed and murdered Lincoln County sheriff William Brady, who was indirectly responsible for the death of Tunstall.

Knowing they were wanted in Lincoln, three days later the men headed out of town to Blazer's Mill, located on a hillside between Lincoln and Tularosa, owned by Dr. Joseph H. Blazer, a dentist. The area included a large two-story house, a square office building, a sawmill, a grist mill, several one-story adobe structures and houses, a post office, a general store, and a number of corrals and barns. The Regulators stopped in for a meal at Mrs. Godfrey's Restaurant. Known to be riding along with Brown that day was a close friend of Billy's, Charlie Bowdre, and also Doc Scurlock, Frank McNab, George Coe, Frank Coe, John Middleton, Jim French, Fred Waite, and several others.

They say timing is everything, and Buckshot Roberts certainly had none. Roberts, who had been on the Murphy-Dolan side, had decided he wanted no part in the feuds and fighting. He had sold his ranch and rode into Blazer's Mill that day to pick up his waiting check. As soon as that was done, he'd head out of the area. Imagine his shock to discover the upper echelon of the Regulators eating in a nearby building. Upon being noticed, Roberts sat with Regulator Frank Coe on the steps of the main house, where Coe tried to talk him into surrendering.

The old gunman refused, believing the vengeful Regulators would kill him. Turns out, he was right. Leader Dick Brewer sent a few of the men to take Roberts into custody. When Roberts spotted Bowdre and another gunman marching his way, he shot. Bowdre's belt buckle took a bullet, severing his gun belt and knocking the wind out of him.

Bullets flew. Severely wounded, Roberts barricaded himself in a house and opened fire when Brewer peeked over a log pile. He shot Brewer in the head. Demoralized by Brewer's death, the Regulators left the area. Roberts died the next day, and in a bizarre twist of fate, he and Brewer were buried side by side near the big house where the gunfight occurred.

The End of the Lincoln County War

Fugitives on the run for the Brady and Roberts murders, the Regulators spent the next several weeks hiding. When they rode back into Lincoln, they found not much had changed. The two sides were still at war. Under fire from Brady's men and Murphy's faction, on July 15, 1878, a handful of Regulators took shelter in Alexander McSween's house, where McSween, his wife, and his children hid. Trapped in the house, the men put up with intermittent gunfire and the threat of interference from the US Army at Fort Stanton. Fortunately, Brown was one of three Regulators not actually in McSween's house just then; he had positioned himself behind the Tunstall store near a grain warehouse. After three days, the army brought in a cannon while the Murphy faction tried to set McSween's adobe house on fire. It took several attempts, but eventually the porch and other wooden portions of the house caught. Mrs. McSween and the children ran out the back, unharmed.

Billy managed to escape with three others, the fourth killed in the melee. McSween, who thought he could walk out and talk sense into the army, was shot down. His death essentially marked the end of the Lincoln County War.

Tascosa

With the Lincoln County War over, the Regulators disbanded and scattered. Brown, who had stolen horses in the Pecos Valley, ran them into the Tascosa area of the Texas Panhandle where horse buyers didn't look too closely at brands. Billy and a few other former Regulators rode along. By October, Billy and best friend Tom O'Folliard were ready to return to New Mexico, even though they were wanted by the law there. Brown, named in two murder warrants in New Mexico, wisely elected to stay in Tascosa for a bit.

A Lawman in Texas

For a while Brown was a cowhand, but he then took a job tracking horse thieves. Around 1880, he drifted into Oldham County, Texas, where he wangled an appointment as a deputy sheriff. He was soon fired because he "was always wanting to fight and get his mane up." In 1881, he went to work again for a cattle outfit but was discharged from that job, too, "because he was always on the war path." A couple months later, he moved to Oklahoma and worked on several cattle ranches in Woods County. By then he was a seasoned gunfighter with a growing taste for the lawman's side of the business. A good and rowdy Kansas cattle town might just quench the thirst.

Moving to Caldwell, Kansas

In July 1882, when Brown was twenty-five, he settled in Caldwell, Kansas—a rough cattle town just across the Kansas line and comparable to Dodge City and Abilene for rowdiness. The Chisholm Trail met the Atchison-Topeka and Santa Fe tracks in Caldwell and, as the terminus of the trail, had a long history of violence.

By late 1882, new to town, Brown was hired as an assistant marshal, his past activities and reputation unknown to the citizens. Within six months the mayor and city council moved him up from assistant marshal to acting marshal to marshal. As marshal, he killed two men—an Indian who tried to resist arrest, and a gambler who had a shoot-out with Brown. But it was Brown's mere presence that mattered most. With his hand-picked deputy—tall, muscled Texan Ben Wheeler—Brown dominated the once-wild streets. The incongruous pair—the diminutive marshal and his towering right-hand man—rarely had to use their guns.

The *Caldwell Post* bragged that Brown was "one of the quickest men on the trigger in the Southwest." The citizens were taken with Brown, who was "very much undersize" but did not drink, gamble, or even smoke or chew tobacco. Plus, he was in regular attendance at the Methodist Church. All this *and* he had removed the town's criminal element. Said to be "exceedingly modest and, in fact, bashful," he appeared reclusive, but "gained the entire confidence of the people . . . and . . . conducted himself in such a manner that the doors of society were always open to him."

In their appreciation, the people presented him with a new Winchester rifle, replacing his old, worn one. Described as elegant, gold-mounted, and handsomely engraved, it had a fancy silver plate bearing an inscription to Brown: "For valuable services rendered. A. N. Colson, Mayor Dec 1882."

The *Caldwell Commercial* lauded him as "cool, courageous and gentlemanly, and free from vices." In early 1884, he married a local woman, Alice Maude Levagood, the daughter of a well-to-do Caldwell brick maker. Alice had a college degree—rare for women of that era.

Apparently she pronounced her name "Lee-va-good," for in announcing the marriage, the *Caldwell Journal* noted the event with a pun: "He did not Lev a good girl at all, but took her unto himself for better or for worse," before adding that the newspaper staff collectively "throws its old shoe after the young folks and wishes them a long and prosperous life."

In a rare move for a Western gunfighter, Brown bought his new bride a house. However, what he failed to mention in his vows was that he had been living beyond his means, and debts were mounting. Brown searched for ways to supplement his income.

Marshal Brown and his assistant kept the town clean, and by the time they were appointed to their third term, the citizens lauded them as the best and most effective team of lawmen the town had ever had. But the bills were piling up.

Winchester presented to Brown from Caldwell, Kansas, grateful citizens.
KANSAS STATE HISTORICAL SOCIETY

DESTINATION: MEDICINE LODGE, OKLAHOMA

Falling back on his old life as a thief and rustler, Brown and his deputy Ben Wheeler hatched a plan. They would ride to Indian Territory (Oklahoma) to "hunt for a murderer." Wink, wink. The Caldwell mayor approved Brown's request for a $1,200 reward on the murderer's head. Marshal Brown and Deputy Wheeler left in pursuit of this dreadful criminal in April 1884.

Along the way, they picked up two Cherokee Strip cowboys, William Smith and John Wesley, and rode to Medicine Lodge, a settlement about fifty-five miles southwest of Caldwell, at the border of Kansas and Indian Territory. Medicine Lodge, a small town, quiet without the rowdy cattle drovers who frequented places along the railroads and trail, had a small bank with no one like Marshal Brown to protect it. According to an account by a local newspaper editor, the village had previously undergone some bad days when "a few swaggering ruffians took virtual possession of the town, howled about the streets and fired their revolvers until their wild and woolly spirits were satisfied and then left unharmed and went unpunished." After that, the editor added, the place became known as a town whose "white-livered inhabitants" ducked into their houses when desperadoes showed up—a perfect place for a bank holdup.

MEDICINE VALLEY BANK ROBBERY

On April 30, 1884, the three outlaws, William Smith staying behind as lookout, entered the bank shortly after it opened. Guns drawn, they demanded cash. When bank president E. W. Payne reached for his gun, he was shot and killed. Though the chief cashier had his hands up, he too was shot. However, in an act of amazing bravery, he staggered to the vault where he managed to close and lock the door. He then collapsed and died.

Efforts now completely thwarted, the gang ditched their plans, mounted their horses, and galloped off. A group of twelve cowboys who happened to be in a stable directly across the street from the bank took off after them, guns blasting. The four outlaws rode, hell-bent for leather . . . right into a box canyon. After a two-hour shoot-out, Brown was first to surrender.

A crowd gathered in Medicine Lodge as the robbers were returned, chanting, "Hang them! Hang them!" The *Caldwell Journal* later reported that a hush then descended on the town, and "the impression prevailed that before many hours the bodies of four murderers would swing in the soft night air."

Once the men were behind bars, the jailers anticipated a lynch mob and offered a meal, took a group photo, and strongly suggested the men write home—pen their final words, so to speak. Brown wrote a poignant letter to his wife of six weeks. It reads in part,

Darling Wife:

I am in jail here. I want you to come and see me as soon as you can. I will send you all of my things, and you can sell them, but keep the Winchester. This is hard for me to write this letter but, it was all for you, my sweet wife, and for the love I have

*for you. Do not go back on me; if you do it will kill me. If a
mob does not kill us we will come out all right after awhile.
Maude, I did not shoot anyone, and did not want the others
to kill anyone; but they did, and that is all there is about it.
Now, good-bye, my darling wife.*

H. N. Brown

Realizing that a lynching was imminent, John Wesley, Brown's
partner in crime, removed his boot. When it slipped off, so did
the leg-iron shackles, which had been attached to Brown. Using
his bandana, Brown tied the loose end of the leg-iron to his leg,
allowing him to run unencumbered. Ben Wheeler was hand-
cuffed to Smith, who slipped the handcuff over his small hand.
Unknown to the gathering crowd, all four were now free.

When the lynch mob came at about nine that evening
and broke into the jail, Brown burst through the startled citizens to an alley alongside the jail. As he ran, both barrels of a
shotgun blasted, hitting him at almost point blank range. He
died instantly. Wheeler ran about a hundred yards before being
wounded. However, he lived long enough to hang on an elm tree
alongside Smith and Wesley. Reports claim that the town was still
angry at Brown, especially because they hadn't had the pleasure of
hanging him. They went ahead and strung him up anyway, then
peppered him with bullets.

With the men hanged, the so-called white-livered inhabitants
of Medicine Lodge went home. Soon afterward the local newspaper wrote, "Mob law is to be deplored under almost any circum-
stance, but in this case the general sentiment of the community
will uphold the summary execution of justice by the taking of
these murderers' lives." The *Medicine Lodge Cresset* summarized
the tragedy as "a murder and attempted bank robbery, which, for
cold-bloodedness and boldness of design, was never exceeded by
the most famous exploits of the James gang."

Naturally, the town of Caldwell was shocked, shattered. "When the news came," the *Journal* reported, "it fell like a thunderbolt at midday. People doubted, wondered, and when the stern facts were at last beyond question, accepted them reluctantly." Henry Newton Brown was twenty-seven when he died.

Afterword

Brown's widow continued to live in Caldwell after his death but ignored his instructions about the Winchester. She gave the gun to acquaintances. The rifle moved to Texas with its new owners and later was finally sold to a gun collector. In 1977 the Winchester was donated to the Kansas Historical Society.

Maude Brown, born in 1861, graduated from Park College in Parkville, Missouri, class of 1882. She taught on an Indian reservation where, on a trip back to Missouri, she rode on a stagecoach with Buffalo Bill Cody. Years after her husband's death, she moved to North Dakota and bought land there. Later, she moved to Indiana where she died in 1935 at age seventy-four. She never remarried.

CHAPTER ELEVEN

Robert (Bob) Olinger: Killed by Billy the Kid

Bob was a murderer from the cradle, and if there is a hell hereafter, then he is there.

—REBECCA OLINGER, BOB'S MOM

ROBERT OLINGER MADE ONE FATAL MISTAKE. HE MADE AN enemy of Billy the Kid. The man Billy looked up to almost as a father figure was Englishman John Tunstall of Lincoln, New Mexico, about five years older than Billy. Tunstall took him under his wing, gave him a job, and guided him. When Olinger killed Tunstall, Billy went gunning. He vowed, "I'll get every son-of-a-bitch who helped kill John, if it's the last thing I do."

EARLY LIFE

Robert Ameredith Olinger was born around March 1850 in Delphi, Indiana, to William C. Olinger and Rebecca Richardson Olinger. They moved to Polk County, Iowa, then to Linn County, Kansas Territory, by 1858. Bob's father died at age thirty-seven in 1861, and his mother married Joshua Stafford. The family moved to Bourbon County, Kansas, in 1865. From there they moved to Oklahoma and then Texas around 1874.

Robert Olinger was deputy
to Sheriff Pat Garrett.
AUTHOR'S COLLECTION

Bob's brother, John, and John's ranching partner moved to Seven Rivers, New Mexico, near Lincoln. Shortly thereafter, Bob and his mother moved there too. In 1876 Bob was appointed marshal of Seven Rivers in Lincoln County. However, the job was short-lived, as he was soon fired when he was suspected of consorting with an outlaw band. Not surprisingly, Olinger had a love of gambling and drinking, often placing him in questionable company.

A KILLING MACHINE

Olinger was never too picky about whom he killed. The first was his friend, Juan Chavez. With no history of violence between them, one evening they were playing poker in the Royal Saloon in Seven Rivers. However, when Chavez accused Olinger of cheating, Olinger stood, leveling his six-shooter at his friend's head. Another player then tossed a gun to the unarmed Chavez, and the two exchanged shots. When the smoke cleared, Chavez lay dead on the floor. Without remorse, Olinger simply looked down at him, stating, "All's well that ends well." He then strode out the door.

"Never gamble with Olinger" should have been on the lips of every man in New Mexico. Another evening, Olinger and a man named John Hill were playing poker, and Olinger quickly won Hill's money. Chagrined and obviously upset, Hill told everyone within earshot not to play cards with Bob Olinger because he would lead them on, allowing them to win a few hands. Then he'd pounce, pulling winning hands out of nowhere, yet doing it so smoothly they wouldn't suspect they'd just been duped.

Hill objected—loudly. But the words seemed to bounce off of Olinger, because he did nothing. He just continued playing cards. When Hill left the saloon later that night, Olinger shot him dead.

Lincoln County War: A Hired Gun

In February 1878, when the Lincoln County War erupted, Olinger was right in the middle of it, working with the Seven Rivers Warriors who supported the Dolan-Murphy group. The Warriors used the town as their refuge.

The Dolan-Murphy faction had obtained a court order to seize some of John Tunstall's horses as payment for an outstanding debt. Tunstall, of course, refused. Lincoln County sheriff William Brady formed a posse to go after Tunstall. Olinger, a hired gun for the James Dolan–Lawrence Murphy faction, was prominent in this group. On February 18, 1878, Tunstall, riding in a lonely ravine near Pajarito Spring, was gunned down in cold blood by Olinger and the gang.

Although several riders participated, only James Dolan and Jacob B. "Billy" Matthews were arrested, charged with being accessories to murder. After being charged with accessory, both Dolan and Matthews received a change of venue to Socorro County in 1879. Acquitted of any wrongdoing, both men returned to society. Olinger was never punished for his well-known part in the death of the unarmed John Tunstall.

QUICK ON THE DRAW

"Pecos Bob," as he styled himself, stirred controversy wherever he went. Bell Hudson described him as "two hundred pounds of bones and muscle, six feet tall, round as a huge tree trunk, with a regular gorilla-like chest that bulged out so far his chin seemed to be set back in his chest . . . shaggy hair, bushy eyebrows and hat-rack mustache. Despite his build and size he was quick as a cat and always got the best of the deal in any encounter he figured in."

As time went on, each of Olinger's killings seemingly increased in violence. One year, when Olinger was playing poker with Bob Jones, as was Olinger's norm, another gambling dispute arose. Jones, who had heard of Olinger's reputation, wisely backed down. However, Olinger saw a chance to aggravate Bob when he found that Deputy Pierce Jones had a misdemeanor warrant to serve on Bob Jones. Olinger decided to tag along, and when they arrived at Bob Jones's home, Jones was working in the yard while his three children played and his wife was in the kitchen.

Offering no resistance, Bob Jones asked the deputy if he could explain to his wife that he would return as soon as he paid his fine. The deputy agreed, and Jones made his way to the house, passing by his hunting gun, which was lying on the porch. Although Jones made no attempt to pick up the rifle, Olinger drew a pistol and fired three shots into his back. Jones's wife and children stood by screaming while Deputy Jones stood shocked. Olinger expressed belief that he could claim self-defense for the outright murder.

Deputy Jones quickly brought murder charges against Olinger, and Lincoln County authorities issued a warrant for his arrest. Sheriff George Kimball arrested him and brought him to Lincoln for trial in October 1879. However, for unknown reasons, the case was dismissed without going to court.

Becoming Sheriff Pat Garrett's Deputy

On November 2, 1880, Patrick Floyd Garrett, who spent as much time in gambling dens as he did upholding the law, was elected to the office of sheriff of Lincoln County. He officially took office in January 1881. Despite many reservations, and much to Garrett's chagrin, Olinger was appointed his deputy. In his autobiography, Garrett said Olinger was a good deputy in some ways but had a bloodthirsty urge for violence.

This urge showed itself in spades when, on one occasion, Garrett and Olinger went to arrest an armed Mexican. Garrett promised the man, who had taken cover in a ditch, that if he surrendered, he would not be hurt. However, as the man came forward with his hands in the air, Olinger drew his pistol, ready to shoot. Garrett placed himself in front of the man, saying to Olinger, "Put it away, Bob. Unless you want to try me."

When a price was put on Billy the Kid's head and acting sheriff Pat Garrett decided to track him down, the swaggering Olinger hoped that it would be he who would kill the famous outlaw. In December 1880, Pat Garrett found outlaws Billy, Dave Rudabaugh, Tom Pickett, and Bill Wilson at an old forage station called Stinking Springs. They were subsequently arrested and taken to Santa Fe, where they would then go by train to stand trial in Mesilla, New Mexico Territory.

Taunting the Kid

After Billy was taken into custody, it was the duty of Olinger and a Santa Fe deputy to put Billy on the southbound train headed to Mesilla. Billy, anchored with heavy weights, sat next to the window. Olinger rode beside him with a shotgun across his lap, a pistol dangling from each hip, and a bowie knife thrust in his belt. All the way to Mesilla, Olinger taunted Billy. "Your days are short, Kid. I can see that rope around your neck now."

In April 1881, after a short deliberation, the jury returned with a guilty verdict in the first-degree murder of William Brady and assessed the death penalty. (More than fifty individuals were indicted for crimes in the Lincoln County War, but only Billy was ever convicted.) The judge ordered Billy hanged in Lincoln on May 13, 1881.

On April 15, the Doña Ana County sheriff turned Billy over to Olinger, who chained Billy to a wagon for his trip back to Lincoln. Concerned that some of Billy's friends would try to rescue him, the sheriff assigned seven heavily armed guards to take him to Lincoln. US deputy marshal Bob Olinger sat facing Billy the entire way. He continually tormented him, poking him with the muzzle of his shotgun, daring him to make a break for it. "Be careful, Bob," Billy quietly retorted, "I'm not hung yet." Olinger jabbed him in the stomach again with his shotgun. A majority of the guards sympathized with Billy, in spite of his reputation as a killer.

Reluctantly, Olinger turned the unharmed Kid over to Garrett along with an expense account for $1,319. The cost of Billy's trial in Mesilla was only eighty dollars. Billy was secreted in the upper northeast section of the old courthouse, a former Murphy store. Olinger never stopped taunting Billy, and Garrett was forced to tell him to "lay off the Kid," while cautioning him and Deputy J. W. Bell to be careful around the prisoner because he was shifty. At one point Olinger placed a pistol on a table within Billy's reach, hoping he would go for it. But Billy didn't take the bait.

It was well known around town that Olinger and Billy hated each other. Olinger held Billy responsible for killing his friend Bob Beckwith in Alexander McSween's backyard on the night of the final shootout of what historians call the Three Day War. On the afternoon of July 15, 1878, the Regulators were positioned in Lincoln in two different areas: the McSween house and the Ellis store. Facing them were the Dolan–Murphy–Seven Rivers cowboys. In the McSween house were Alex McSween, his wife Susan,

Rare photo of Lincoln County Deputies Bob Olinger and James Bell. Both killed by Billy the Kid.
AUTHOR'S COLLECTION

Billy the Kid, Henry Brown, Jim French, Tom O'Folliard, Jose Chavez y Chavez, George Coe, and a dozen Mexican vaqueros.

Over the next three days, the men exchanged shots and shouts. On the afternoon of July 19, the Murphy-Dolan faction set the house on fire. As the flames spread and night fell, Susan McSween and the other woman and five children were granted safe passage out of the house, while the men inside continued to fight the fire. Billy the Kid and three others ran from the house, drawing fire, while the others escaped. The Dolan men spotted them running and opened fire, killing McSween's law partner. Troopers moved into the backyard when a close-quarters gunfight erupted. Alexander McSween and the Seven Rivers cowboy Bob Beckwith both died.

According to an acquaintance, Olinger declared that the Kid "was a cur and that every man he had killed had been murdered in cold blood and without the slightest chance of defending himself." Even Pat Garrett weighed in. "There was a reciprocal hatred between those two, and neither attempted to disguise or conceal his antipathy for the other."

"... AND HE'S KILLED ME TOO"

On April 28, 1881, Garrett rode to the village of White Oaks to collect taxes—part of a lawman's job—and left Olinger and Deputy James Bell to watch over Billy and the five other prisoners. As Garrett gave final instructions, Deputy Bell and Billy, who had a cell by himself upstairs, were playing poker through the iron bars. At 5 p.m., Olinger walked his five other prisoners a block away to the Wortley Hotel for supper, leaving Bell behind with Billy.

According to Garrett's account from eyewitnesses, Billy asked to be escorted to the privy out back. Deputy James Bell, who was always kind to Billy and seemed to like him, relaxed, even though Garrett had given specific instructions not to let his guard down.

According to Garrett's account, as Billy and Bell returned from the privy, Billy walked quickly, putting a good distance between them. Billy turned on the landing of stairs, hidden from the deputy. Light and active, Billy bounded up the stairs, turned to his right, put his shoulder to the door of the armory room, entered, seized a six-shooter, and returned to the head of the stairs just as Bell faced him on the landing some twelve steps beneath. Bell fired at Billy. Billy returned fire, striking the deputy. Bell turned, running out into the corral and toward the gate. He fell dead before reaching it.

Billy ran to Garrett's office and grabbed Olinger's breech-loading double-barreled shotgun. As Garrett wrote in his book, "Olinger had loaded it that morning, in the presence of the Kid, putting eighteen buckshot in each barrel, and remarked, 'The man that gets one of those loads will feel it.'"

From the Wortley Hotel, Olinger heard the shots, jumped to his feet, and assumed Billy had been killed. Furious he wasn't the one who'd had the pleasure of killing Billy, Olinger ran outside, his prisoners trailing into the street. He cut along the east wall and bumped into Godfrey Gauss, the cook for the Tunstall hands who knew Billy well. Gauss said, "Bob, the Kid has killed Bell."

Olinger looked up at Billy who, shotgun in hand, leaned out the second-story window. Olinger replied, "Yes, and he's killed me too." Billy gazed down at the deputy who was directly under the courthouse window and called to him, "Hello, old boy." He unloaded both barrels.

Olinger fell dead, his shoulders and chest riddled. He had just turned thirty-one.

The bodies of deputies Bob Olinger and James Bell were placed in a room in the corral behind the courthouse and remained there until Garrett returned. Olinger is buried at the back of the Fort Stanton cemetery. When he returned, Garrett swore to make Billy pay, which he did on July 14, 1881. Or did he?

ALWAYS THE "WHAT IFS"

When Billy escaped, why didn't he gallop across the few hundred miles of sparsely settled country that separated Lincoln from Mexico, where he would have been safe from pursuit? He spoke Spanish like a native. He was well liked and would have gotten along well. And he had a good start on his pursuers. Why not? Was it because of his love, Paulita Maxwell? We'll never know for sure.

In Robert Utley's book *Billy the Kid: A Short and Violent Life*, he writes, "Kid said of this killing [of Bell], 'I did not want to kill Bell, but I had to do so in order to save my own life. It was a case of have to, not wanting to.'"

Area near the courthouse where Olinger was shot.
AUTHOR'S COLLECTION

IN MEMORIAM

Deputy Robert Olinger is memorialized at Panel 13, W-3, on the National Law Enforcement Officers Memorial in Washington, DC.

Chapter Twelve

Elfego Baca:
America's Longest Gunfight

I will show the Texans there is at least one Mexican in the country who is not afraid of an American cowboy.
—Elfego Baca, 1884

In a dramatic display of skill, nerve, and pure dumb luck, an unimposing five-foot-seven Hispanic man by the name of Elfego Baca instigated and prevailed in what was likely the most unequal civilian gunfight in American West history. It was definitely the most unusual. The Frisco Shootout was the largest and longest gunfight in history.

THE FRISCO SHOOTOUT

Long before Anglo miners and trappers explored the area in what is now middle western New Mexico, the land supported several hundred Spanish-speaking families. Farming, fishing, and hunting kept the people well fed. Before them, Apache, Pima, and other Indian tribes had lived there since the 1200s.

In the 1880s, cattlemen arrived from Texas and Oklahoma, swelling the population of the town of Middle San Francisco Plaza (now Reserve, New Mexico) on a daily basis. By 1884 it had become the staging ground for the last of the Indian wars. Anglos sparred with Hispanics who sparred with Indians. Added to that mixture were heated arguments between the various cattle outfits—men who "rode for the brand" and took offense when someone from another ranch made an offhand comment. But even this did not keep more than a dozen saloons and bordellos from springing up in the villages of Middle and Lower Frisco. The valley became rife with tension.

The Hispanic residents of Frisco were being harassed by the cowboys, in particular those of the nearby John Slaughter ranch. Town sheriff Pedro Sarracino sought help. In October 1884, it arrived in the form of his friend, nineteen-year-old Elfego Baca of Socorro, 130 miles away. The Slaughter cowboys numbered more than 150. Rather full of teenaged hutzpah, gumption, and stupidity, Baca agreed to help his friend, proclaiming, "I will show the Texans there is at least one Mexican in the country who is not afraid of an American cowboy."

According to one story, as soon as Baca arrived, Sheriff Sarracino deputized him. However, Baca claimed in his memoirs that he had actually purchased a child's tin star and appointed himself law. Whether or not he was an honest-to-goodness lawman at this point, his long ride southwest set in motion a series of events that became known as the Frisco War.

It did not take Baca long to make his first and only arrest. An Irish-blooded army vet saloon owner pointed to a drunken cowboy, Charlie McCarty, who was waving his pistol at Mexicans in the saloon, making them dance. Baca flashed his badge at McCarty and took his gun. His prisoner hailed from a notoriously rowdy outfit at the John B. Slaughter ranch across the Arizona border. The other cowboys were none too happy to hear that this swaggering, self-appointed hero had snagged their boy. A standoff with the cowboys ensued. The number of men who gathered has been disputed, with villagers at the scene reporting about forty, while Baca himself later claimed there had been at least eighty.

By this time, the cowboys, still liquored up and ready to fight, had gathered with their Winchester rifles at the ready. The leader of this "mob" was Slaughter Ranch foreman Young Parham. Yelling into the blockaded saloon, they demanded McCarty's release, testing the door and windows with their shoulders. They'd take him by force if necessary. Baca responded from inside, threatening to shoot if they weren't "out of there by the count of three." The story goes that the ranch hands were in the process of making jokes about Baca's type "being unable to count" when they heard Baca call out in a single quick breath: "One-two-three!" He and his friends and "deputies" who were holed up inside began shooting through the door.

In the resulting hail of lead, Young Parham had his horse shot out from under him. The horse fell dead, crushing and killing Parham in its fall. Another cowboy was shot, a bullet through his knee. Out of ammunition and looking to take care of Parham, his horse, and the wounded man, the ranch hands retreated, swearing vengeance at Baca and his trapped deputies.

Still inside the saloon, Baca received a signed agreement that he would be left alone if his prisoner could be tried the following day at Milligan's bar. He reluctantly agreed.

The next day, a quick "trial" took place, and the now-sober cowboy, McCarty, was fined five dollars. The justice of the peace ordered his release. But by now Anglo cowboys from nearby ranches had heard Hispanics were going on rampages, killing and dismembering whites in Frisco. As they say, all hell had broken loose. After giving more thought to the situation, the justice summoned Bert Hearne, a rancher from Spur Lake Ranch, to bring Baca back to the justice of the peace in Socorro for questioning and possible arrest relating to the murder of John Slaughter's foreman.

Not willing to be arrested or mobbed, Baca slipped out a side door of the bar, running for his life and taking refuge in a nearby jacal (a single-story adobe structure created out of mesquite sticks and dried mud, with walls that do not stop bullets) belonging to Geronimo Armijo. Counts vary, but the cowboys fired more than four thousand shots into the house, until the adobe building was full of holes. Incredibly, not one of the bullets struck Baca. After Baca refused to come out of the adobe jacal, Hearne broke down the door and ordered Baca to come out with his hands up. Immediately, shots volleyed from the jacal and hit Hearne in the stomach. He died within moments.

While most of the town climbed up on the overlooking hills to watch, a group of the attackers stretched blankets between the nearby houses to conceal their movements, and others fired from behind the buttress of the adobe church. A siege on Baca soon began, with between forty and one hundred cowboys firing into the jacal. In the gunplay that took place, three other cowboys were killed (some historians believe Hearne was the only fatality) and eight were wounded. That evening a lit stick of dynamite was tossed into the jacal and set the structure on fire, causing a wall and the roof collapse. Surely Baca was dead. How could it be otherwise? The cowboys decided to investigate the carnage soberly, in the light of day. Tomorrow.

As the sun peeked over the Mogollon Rim, the cowboys who'd spent the night sleeping on the cold ground around Baca's hideout awoke to the smell of coffee boiling and fresh tortillas cooking. Baca had fixed his breakfast before continuing the war. The battle started all over. One hungry and enraged cowboy charged forward using a cast-iron shield made from a cook stove, but he dropped it when a slug creased his hairline.

Before Baca agreed to cease and desist, he insisted that he stand trial in his hometown of Socorro and that he retain his two pistols (one was McCarty's) while riding in the back of a buckboard on the trip there. Trailing cowboys were not allowed to come within thirty feet.

In all, the siege of Baca's hiding place lasted thirty-three hours until he officially surrendered at six in the evening. An estimated four thousand rounds had poured into the home, but astonishingly, a plaster statue of Nuestra Señora Doña Ana escaped unscathed, as did Baca. The fact that he survived at all was considered a miracle, until his secret was discovered. The jacal's floor was recessed almost a foot and a half, allowing Baca to lie beneath the rain of bullets sent his way.

On the way back to Socorro, Baca, who seemed to lead a charmed life, also missed an ambush planned for him en route. Two different groups of retaliators each mistakenly thought the other had carried out an attack. Surely Baca was dead, they figured, or at least gravely wounded. He arrived in Socorro totally unscathed.

Elfego Baca at 19, when he survived a 33-hour siege resulting in over 4,000 rounds of open fire.
CENTER FOR SOUTHWEST RESEARCH

In May 1885, Baca was officially charged with murder for the death of John Slaughter's foreman, and Bert Hearne and was jailed awaiting trial. In August of that year, Baca was acquitted. With more than four hundred bullet holes, the door of Armijo's house, entered as evidence, was proof positive of the blazing gunfight.

EARLY YEARS

Many legends surround Elfego Baca, but a few facts are certain. On February 10, 1865, he was born in Socorro, New Mexico, to Francisco and Juana Maria Baca. Legend 1: His mother was said to have been playing the Mexican version of softball, Las Iglesias, when the future lawman arrived—on the field. Legend 2: Baca was kidnapped at age one by Indians but was immediately returned to his family when his screaming disturbed the silence of the abductor's camp.

Baca moved with his family to Topeka, Kansas, where, surrounded by Anglos, he learned about confrontation—using his wits before resorting to fists or gunplay, but never backing down. Yet another legend says that at age twelve, Baca helped his father escape jail by sawing through the ceiling of his cell. Baca Sr. had been charged with killing two men in a mob that threatened to lynch a prisoner. When his mother died in 1880—along with a sister and brother—from a plague infecting the region, young Baca and his father headed back to New Mexico, settling in the town of Belen, north of Socorro. Baca Sr. became a marshal in Belen.

LAW AND ORDER EVERY TIME

Famous as a hardcase law-and-order man, Baca used his notoriety from the Frisco gun battle to work a variety of jobs. Marc Simmons wrote, "Baca was not only a man of lionlike courage, reputed to have killed seven men in stand-up fights, but he was also endowed with intellect and resourcefulness."

Baca officially became the sheriff of Socorro County and secured indictments for the arrest of the area's lawbreakers. Baca began his law career as a deputy sheriff of Socorro, eighty miles south of Albuquerque. Instead of ordering his deputies to pursue the wanted men, he sent each of the accused a letter. It read, "I have a warrant here for your arrest. Please come in by [a certain date] and give yourself up. If you don't, I'll know you intend to resist arrest, and I will feel justified in shooting you on sight when I come after you." Most of the offenders turned themselves in voluntarily.

First a Lawman, Then a Lawyer

In 1888, Baca became a US marshal. He served two years and then studied law. In December 1894, he was admitted to the bar and briefly joined Freeman's law firm in Socorro in February 1895. He later practiced law on San Antonio Street in El Paso, Texas, between 1902 and 1904.

Another legend: Once when he was practicing law in Albuquerque, Baca received a telegram from a client in El Paso. "Need you at once," it read. "Have just been charged with murder." Baca supposedly responded with a telegram saying, "Leaving at once with three eyewitnesses."

Political Life

Baca held a number of public offices in succession, including county clerk, mayor and school superintendent of Socorro County, and district attorney for Socorro and Sierra Counties. In his book *The Shooters*, Baca's biographer, Leon Metz writes, "Most reports say he was the best peace officer Socorro ever had."

Bigger Than Life

Metz also wrote, "Elfego was, and is, controversial. He drank too much; talked too much. He had a weakness for wild women. He was often arrogant and, of course, he showed no compunction about killing people."

In 1910, according to Albuquerque historian Marc Simmons, Baca moved to Albuquerque to make his way as a lawyer and private detective. In William Keleher's book *Memoirs*, he says, "Dressed in a flowing cape and trailed by a bodyguard, he stalked the downtown streets handing out business cards that read on one side: 'Elfego Baca, Attorney-at-Law, Fees Moderate,' and on the other side, 'Private Detective; Divorce Investigations Our Specialty, Discreet Shadowing Done.'"

When New Mexico became a state in 1912, Baca unsuccessfully ran for Congress. Nevertheless, he remained a valued political figure because of his ability to turn out the vote among the Hispanic population. As if being a private detective wasn't exciting enough, Baca took a job as a bouncer in a casino across the border in Ciudad Juárez, Mexico.

Courtroom Antics

From 1913 to 1916, Baca served as the official US representative of Victoriano Huerta's government during the Mexican Revolution. The Republic of Mexico had endured unremitting political turmoil and civil war. Victoriano Huerta had finally wrested control of the presidency, but he continued to face challenges to the central government posed by guerrilla leaders in the northern provinces. Chief among them was Pancho Villa, who controlled much of the state of Chihuahua, bordering New Mexico. With the Villistas closing in, in early January 1914, Mexican general José Inés Salazar, a Huerta backer, crossed into the United States. Almost at once he was arrested and charged with violating American neutrality laws. Placed in military custody, the general was taken to Fort Wingate, near Gallup, for incarceration.

There, Salazar met Baca, who had been engaged by the Huerta government to act as the general's legal counsel. President Huerta wanted Salazar out of jail and back in Mexico. Baca went to Washington but failed to persuade the release of Salazar. Surprisingly, on November 16, 1914, Salazar was transferred to the Bernalillo County jail in Albuquerque. Four days later, he escaped. Coincidence? Many think not. According to the rumor mill, two of Huerta's secret agents had come to town, quietly made contact with certain local residents, and provided them with substantial funds to arrange Salazar's freedom. Some believed that Elfego Baca and Manuel Vigil, Bernalillo County district attorney, were ringleaders. However, both had ironclad alibis for their whereabouts that fateful night. Baca was drinking with a large crowd at the Graham Bar in downtown Albuquerque, while Vigil was in Gallup, more than 160 miles away.

The following April 1915, a grand jury handed down indictments to Baca, along with Vigil and four others, charging them with being conspirators in the freeing of José Salazar. At their trial in December, they were all acquitted. Baca's reputation grew among Southwestern residents.

Baca worked closely with New Mexico's longtime senator Bronson Cutting as a political investigator and wrote a weekly column in Spanish praising Cutting's work on behalf of local Hispanics. Baca considered running for governor despite his declining health, but he failed to secure the Democratic Party's nomination for district attorney in 1944.

On his seventy-fifth birthday, Baca told the *Albuquerque Tribune* that as a lawyer he had defended thirty people charged with murder and only one went to the penitentiary.

A LEGEND IN HIS OWN MIND—AND EVERYONE ELSE'S

For slightly over eighty years, Elfego Baca remained a lively part of New Mexico's cultural landscape, telling spirited stories of cagey señoritas and political intrigue to anyone with the time to listen. He was one of those who started life at the end of the Civil War and died at the end of World War II.

But it was the Frisco Shootout that earned Baca his lifelong reputation as one tough hombre. This reputation would follow

This bronze statue was erected in Reserve, New Mexico, in 2007.

him throughout his years as a flamboyant criminal lawyer, school superintendent, district attorney, chief bouncer of a Prohibition era gambling house in Juarez, and the American agent for General Huerta during the convoluted Mexican Revolution.

He died on August 27, 1945, at age eighty, and is buried at Sunset Memorial Park in Albuquerque.

THE AFTERLIFE

Initiated in 1960 and still going strong, the annual Elfego Baca Golf Shootout, held the first week in June, was established by New Mexico Tech University in Socorro. On the course, there is only one hole—a fifty-foot circle chalked in the desert—that is three miles and roughly three thousand feet below a mountain tee box. Each competitor is allowed ten balls and must finish with at least one. They can tee up each shot they take, and they are allowed three ball spotters. Heat, mine shafts, mountain lions, and rattlesnakes constitute some of the "course's" hazards. The course record is nine strokes, and some competitors have taken over eight hours to finish their round.

In 2007, a life-size bronze statue of Baca in action was erected in Reserve, the town he made famous, and dedicated to a man who once held off forty—or four hundred—enraged cowboys. That part is *not* a legend.

Chapter Thirteen

John Henry Selman: The Man Who Killed John Wesley Hardin

We are devils come from Hell!
—A member of Selman's Scouts

Despite Billy the Kid's absence from Lincoln, New Mexico, in the fall of 1878 (Billy was busy "wrangling" horses in Tascosa, Texas), there had been a dramatic uptick in violence, most of it perpetuated by former members of the Murphy-Dolan faction. By far the worst violence was initiated by Selman's Scouts, sometimes called the Rustlers or the Warriors, led by John Henry Selman, a Texas deputy turned desperado. True to their name, they raided cattle herds and horse remudas across the county. They also committed murder and rape, burned down ranches, and pillaged homes and businesses in Lincoln and elsewhere. One of Selman's gang members told a bystander, "We are devils come from Hell!" Of that there was no doubt.

Early Life and Service with the Confederacy
The son of Englishman Jeremiah Selman, John Henry Selman was born November 16, 1839, in Madison County, Arkansas, the sixth child of the Selman family. The Selmans moved to Grayson

County, Texas, in 1858. The senior Selman died in December 1861, at which time John joined the 22nd Regiment of the Texas Cavalry stationed at Fort Washita, Oklahoma. He fought as a private in the Civil War. However, just fifteen months after enlisting, he deserted Fort Washita in April 1863. He picked up his mother, brothers, and sisters and moved to Fort Davis, a Stephens County settlement near the fort on the Clear Fork of the Brazos River. There he ranched, farmed, and fought Indians.

He also enlisted in the Stephens County Company of Texas State Troops. He must have done well in this regiment, as the following year he was promoted to lieutenant. A few months after his promotion, Selman married Edna Degraffenreid on August 17, 1865. Over the years, the couple had four children. Selman moved his family to Colfax County, New Mexico, where the 1870 census shows he worked as a laborer and was married with two children, John Jr. and William.

Two years later, he returned to Shackleford County, Texas, and ranched near Fort Griffin. Soon afterward, Selman was accused of killing two Native Americans. He joined a group of vigilantes known as the Old Law Mob, later changed to the Tin Hat Brigade.

"Babylon on the Brazos"—Fort Griffin

Fort Griffin during the 1870s was a rowdy, lawless place, filled with a number of notable characters that Selman no doubt came in contact with. Fort Griffin, also known as the Flat, enjoyed a reputation as having "a man for breakfast every morning." The frontier community sat at the crossroads of two major cattle trails that converged below a bluff. The military wisely chose to establish a fort on top of the bluff in 1867, because between the Indian wars and the rowdy cattle drives, the area was rife with tension. In the raucous settlement that earned the title "Babylon on the Brazos" were the characters of Doc Holliday, Wyatt Earp,

John Henry Selman killed famed gunman John Wesley Hardin. Photo probably taken in El Paso around 1894.

Bat Masterson, Big Nose Kate, "Dirty" Dave Rudabaugh, gambler Lottie Deno, Pat Garrett, and John Wesley Hardin.

By 1874, rancher John M. Larn had joined the Fort Griffin Tin Hat Brigade, the self-appointed group of citizens who were fed up with the lawlessness and who had determined swift "justice" was more effective than waiting for "real" law. Soon, many a horse thief was found hanging from a tree near the river. Larn gained much respect as a member of this esteemed group, which helped get him elected sheriff of Fort Griffin in April 1876. Larn resigned as sheriff the following year. In 1877, Selman became a deputy inspector for hides, working under Larn, close friend, fellow inspector, fellow Tin Hatter, and now ex–Shackleford County sheriff.

LIFE AS AN OUTLAW

Inspector John Larn, however, possessed another side. Shortly after taking the sheriff's position, Larn entered into a private contract with the fort to deliver three steers per day. Larn had no intention of filing these contracts legally. When Selman came on board, the pair rustled cattle from neighboring ranches, leaving Larn's entire herd untouched. Before long, Larn and Selman, instead of controlling the area crime, controlled the vigilantes, rustling even more cattle and otherwise terrorizing the county.

Suspicions were soon raised as a number of ranchers noticed that while their herds were slowly shrinking, Larn's grew. Larn and Selman then moved to outright cattle rustling. The pair turned violent—driving off cattle, shooting horses, and firing potshots at the homes of terrified citizens.

Finally, when people found six hides of questionable brands that did not belong to Larn behind his house, the police issued an arrest warrant. In June 1878, Sheriff William Cruger, who had replaced Larn, arrested his former boss. He was taken to the Fort Griffin jail, where Cruger had the local blacksmith shackle Larn to the cell floor to prevent a breakout by the former sheriff's supporters. Instead, the next night, the Tin Hat Brigade, the best-known and probably the most active vigilante committee in Texas, stormed the jail. Former friendships pushed aside, they intended to hang their former member. When they found they couldn't string up the shackled man, they shot him nine times in his cell. Frontier justice at its finest. Although Selman was out of town at the time, he was implicated in the theft and found himself a wanted man, hunted by the same vigilantes he had considered friends.

SELMAN'S SCOUTS/WARRIORS/RUSTLERS

Wisely, Selman disappeared, landing in lawless Lincoln County, New Mexico. There, he and his brother Tom, known as "Tom Cat," formed a gang of vicious outlaws called Selman's Scouts. Selman's gang included Edward "Little" Hart. Later that year, Selman killed Hart in a dispute over who should be leader. Over the next months, Selman and his group were responsible for the murders of six men.

For two months, in September and October 1878, the Scouts rustled horses and cattle, murdered innocent men and boys, and pillaged businesses and homes. In 1879 New Mexico governor Lew Wallace threatened martial law but also issued an amnesty proclamation. The amnesty included almost everyone—except Selman and his Scouts. When it looked as if "real" law was coming to town, the gang broke up. However, no charges were ever filed against Selman there.

By 1880, the Scouts, driven from Lincoln County, had simply moved their operations to Jeff Davis County, Texas. There, at Fort Davis, Selman developed a full-blown case of smallpox. Surviving, he carried severe scars for the rest of his life. Not long after this, Selman was captured by a Texas Ranger and taken back to Albany, Shackelford County, to stand trial for his previous crimes.

Things started to deteriorate for Selman. By now, his brother Tom had been apprehended and lynched by the Tin Hat Brigade somewhere near or in Albany, Texas. Then Selman's wife died while giving birth to a fifth child, a stillborn. The two younger children were placed in the custody of his wife's niece, never to see their father again.

Knowing the law was "hot on his trail," Selman married a Hispanic girl and fled with her and his two oldest boys to Chihuahua, Mexico. There, he and his family hid until around 1888. At some point—records are not clear—his second wife died. Once his name was cleared and all charges against him were dropped, he relaxed.

Acme Saloon, downtown El Paso, Texas, where Selman killed John Hardin.
COURTESY BERNIE SARGENT, EL PASO HISTORY ALLIANCE

And Finally—El Paso

From Chihuahua, in 1888 he and the boys moved north across the border to El Paso, Texas, where he made his living primarily as a gambler and sometimes as a city constable. On August 23, 1893, the fifty-four-year-old Selman married sixteen-year-old Romula Granadine.

On April 5, 1894, Selman killed a former Texas Ranger, Bass (pronounced Baz) Outlaw. Outlaw had recently been fired due to his drinking and threats he had made against a local judge. Selman, encountering the inebriated Outlaw, suggested that the ex-Ranger go home and sober up. When Outlaw refused the suggestion, the two instead walked to Tillie Howard's, a local brothel Outlaw favored. Selman sat in the parlor, waiting. Outlaw fired a shot in the bathroom, scaring everyone. Tillie rushed into the backyard blowing her police whistle, while Outlaw pursued her and tried to take it away.

Texas Ranger Joe McKidrict, who was in the neighborhood, ran to see about the commotion and then attempted to break up the conflict. Outlaw shot him in the back and then in the head, killing him instantly. Just then, Constable Selman reached the back porch, jumped off, and fired at Outlaw. Outlaw returned fire, nearly striking Selman in the face. The gunpowder burned Selman's eyes. He staggered back, screaming, "I can't see, I can't see." Outlaw fired again, hitting Selman above the right knee, severing an artery. Sight blurry, eyes burning, Selman shot again, hitting the drunken man just above the heart. Outlaw then lurched into the street, where he surrendered to another Texas Ranger. Outlaw died four hours later. John Selman, who could not see well for the rest of his life due to the powder burns and who walked with a limp, was then put on trial for killing Outlaw. The judge instructed the jury to find him not guilty.

The Killing of John Wesley Hardin

John Jr., Selman's son who was an El Paso police officer, arrested the mistress of infamous gunman John Wesley Hardin, who was at the time an El Paso attorney. Beluah M'rose (or "the widow M'Rose") had been charged with "brandishing a gun in public" and being drunk and disorderly. She paid a fifty-dollar fine. Hardin, obviously upset, confronted the younger Selman over the arrest, and the two men "had words." In some accounts, supported by members of Selman's family, Hardin actually pistol-whipped "Young John" and threatened his life.

Upon hearing this, "Old John" (thus named to distinguish him from "Young John" Selman) argued with Hardin on San Antonio Street on the afternoon of August 19, 1895. Hardin indicated he had no gun. That night, Hardin went to the Acme Saloon, on the corner of San Antonio and Utah Streets. He passed Old John sitting on a barrel near the doorway. Hardin spent the evening rolling dice. Shortly before midnight, Selman walked into the saloon, drawing his gun at the door. He walked up behind Hardin and fired four quick shots, shooting him in the back of the head, killing him instantly. Selman was arrested, charged with murder, and stood trial. He testified that he had observed Hardin glancing in a mirror and had seen him enter. Hardin then went for his gun. Selman swore he fired in self-defense. On February 12, 1896, the jury announced itself hung. Selman was released on bond, pending retrial.

A Final Gunfight

While out on bond, on the night of April 5, 1896, Selman was playing cards with US deputy marshal George Scarborough, a man Selman had known for years. Some reports say the men argued about Selman's killing of Bass Outlaw, two years ago to the day. However, most say that wasn't the case at all, as Outlaw was not liked—in fact, no one had attended his funeral. Most likely it was because twenty-one-year-old Young John had fallen in love with a fifteen-year-old Mexican girl whose father, an ambassador, disapproved. The young couple had decided to elope to Juarez and get married there. When they could not locate a priest, they opted for a hotel instead. When her mother discovered what was happening, she called the Juarez chief of police, who searched all the hotels until he found the couple. Young John went to jail. The girl went home.

John Hardin, pictured with his 1851 Navy Colt, was the son of a Methodist preacher.
AUTHOR'S COLLECTION

Four days later, on April 5, 1896, Old John, worried about his son being in a Juarez jail, left the upstairs room of the Wigwam Saloon, took a stairway down into the alley, and met up with US deputy marshal Scarborough. He asked him to help spring Young John from the jail across the border. Scarborough, a cautious type, refused, which angered Selman. According to Scarborough's testimony, both men left the alley, where Selman then drew on him first. Scarborough shot in self-defense. Scarborough returned to the saloon alone.

John Henry Selman died early in the morning of April 6, 1896. He was fifty-six. Soon afterward, Scarborough was arrested for murder because no gun was found on Selman's body. Just before Scarborough's trial, though, a thief was arrested, and during the process, police discovered that the gun he had belonged to Selman. The man explained that he had witnessed the shooting and then had stolen Selman's gun before the crowd arrived. Scarborough was acquitted of murder charges and released.

Afterword

Selman was originally buried in an unmarked grave in the Catholic section of El Paso's Concordia Cemetery. News reports of the day clearly stated that the burial was in the Catholic section. His grave marker, however, was placed in the middle of the Protestant section. To date, his exact grave location in the cemetery is unknown.

George Scarborough himself was mortally wounded in a gunfight with two robbers and died on April 5, 1900, exactly four years after he shot John Selman. Young John broke out of the Juarez jail on May 7, 1896, and made his way across the Rio Grande into El Paso. He never saw his sweetheart again, as her mother immediately sent her to Mexico City. He joined the army and was wounded in the Philippines. In 1937, at the age of sixty-seven, he was playing cards with friends in Texas when he suddenly stood straight up and shouted, "O Lord, I don't want to die!" and fell dead across the card table.

Chapter Fourteen

Wyatt Berry Stapp Earp: Arrested for "Keeping and Being Found in a House of Ill-Repute"

Forget what you saw at the movies . . . the facts are more interesting than the legend.
—New York Times

Earp was so long-lived that he managed the unique experience of going to a movie that featured himself.
—Kyle Climans, Fascinate.com

MANY PEOPLE IN MANY WAYS HAVE INTERPRETED THE STORY OF Wyatt Earp, perhaps because of the very different, albeit true, labels applied to him—lawman and outlaw. Much has been written about Earp—hundreds, if not thousands, of articles, books, movies, and stage plays have filled stores, houses, and television sets. The legend has been done to death, as they say. Like Billy the Kid, Wyatt Earp has been dissected, analyzed, questioned, examined, and put back together. What makes Earp different from the Kid is that Earp had a solid foot in the law side of life. Billy? Not so much.

After all this exposure of his life, the facts and legends have divided historians and Old West aficionados into two factions: Those who believe Wyatt Earp was an honest-to-a-fault lawman who did everything he could to see justice served every time, and those who believe that Wyatt Earp, while meaning well and trying to put food on the table, stepped outside the law's boundaries, making him . . . dare we say . . . an outlaw.

LOS ANGELES

In 1911, Wyatt Earp and his common-law wife, Josephine, also known as Sadie, were living in Los Angeles. Those were the days before Social Security, before people living long enough to "retire." If you hadn't socked away money for a "rainy day," then you continued working or finding ways to make money until you didn't need it anymore.

Stuart Lake, Earp's biographer, often told the story of Earp's friend, Bat Masterson. Bat wore his Colt crossdraw style, butt forward and covered, making it almost impossible for anyone to disarm him from behind. Known for his gun skills and propensity to use his weapon to quell any violence, he was constantly pestered by New York gun collectors to sell his famous Colt. Unwilling to do so, and fed up with saying no, Masterson bought an old gun, carved out twenty-two notches (there's no solid evidence Bat actually carved notches into his own gun), and sold it to an ecstatic collector. Fiction or not, Earp and Masterson seemed okay with taking advantage of someone's gullibility.

That's exactly what he was doing in July 1911 when he was caught and publicly embarrassed. The Los Angeles newspapers told the story of a clever scheme to bilk Los Angeles real estate agent J. Y. Peterson out of $2,500. Three men attempted to lure Peterson into a room at the Auditorium Hotel for a rigged faro game. In an attempt to get money from the big San Francisco syndicate that backed the game, Peterson was to purchase $2,500 in chips, then leave when his pile reached $4,000. The three men told him they were angry with the San Francisco group, which paid them only ten dollars a day for running a game that netted hundreds of dollars. Peterson was told that the "sharps" (a person who cheats at cards in order to win money) would prick the cards in the middle so they could see the cards underneath, then make sure he left a winner. Peterson went to the practice session and then the police.

The bunco men booked were E. Dunn, Walter Scott, and W. W. Stapp. It quickly became clear who Stapp actually was. The *Los Angeles Times* reported, "Earp, who in addition to being known by the police as a professional gambler and all-around sharper, has made his headquarters here several years. He was a prominent figure here during the days when racing thrived." Two newspapers ran the story on an inside page, while the *Los Angeles Herald* ran it on the front page on top of the fold. The headline: "Detectives Trap Wyatt Earp, 'Gun Man' in Swindle." An accompanying article called Earp "the noted western 'gun man' and survivor of the famous Earp-Clanton feud" and laced into the old marshal: "Earp, who since race track gambling became a dead letter in California, is alleged to have devoted his time to fleecing the unwary in card games here, conceived the plot, it is declared."

In a rather strange twist of fate, the police realized the next day that they hadn't actually broken up a con game. They'd swooped in before a card had been tossed. Charges were reduced to conspiracy to violate the laws prohibiting gambling, a misdemeanor that would be heard in police court. Earp was released on five hundred dollars bail.

One thing was certain about Earp—he considered himself a gambler far more than a lawman. In fact, he spent most of his years turning cards and running a faro layout, and just a few years toting a badge.

Wyatt Earp, about age 39, probably taken in California. AUTHOR'S COLLECTION

THE EARLY YEARS

One of at least eight children, Wyatt Berry Stapp Earp was born March 19, 1848, in Manmouth, Illinois. Parents Nicholas and Virginia Earp named him after Nicholas's cavalry regiment commander, whom he served under during the Mexican American War in 1846. Earp's siblings were Morgan, Virgil, Warren, James, Virginia, Adelia, and Martha (who died at ten). Earp also had a half brother, Newton, from his father's first marriage. Nicholas Porter Earp was strong-willed, opinionated, often profane, and at times belligerent. While he was generous to neighbors, he was slow to pay his bills. Virginia Ann Cooksey Earp was a gentle, kind woman. Apparently Wyatt inherited qualities from both sides.

During the Civil War, brothers Newton, James, and Virgil joined the Union. Dad Nicholas was a recruiter and trainer. Wyatt wanted to join, too. He left home ready and willing to enlist—best laid plans best laid plans and so forth. He ran into his father, who promptly took him home, making him promise he would not enlist without his mother's permission. He was thirteen.

In 1863 brother James Earp returned home. Nicholas did not like the direction the war was taking, so he decided to move the family to California. Arriving there, they developed a ranch where Wyatt decided ranching didn't suit him. Wyatt found jobs working for freighting outfits hauling loads to Salt Lake City, Utah, and Prescott, Arizona.

In the spring of 1868, the Earps moved east again to Lamar, Missouri, where Nicholas became the local constable. Wyatt rejoined the family the next year. When Nicholas resigned in November 1869 to become justice of the peace, Wyatt was appointed constable in his place.

Wyatt Earp moved often and spent time in Pella, Iowa. In 1870, he married Urilla Sutherland, daughter of a hotel keeper. She contracted typhoid fever and died shortly before bearing their first child.

LIVING THE OUTLAW LIFE

Blinded by grief, for the next two years Wyatt Earp's life was one poor decision after another. Apparently he had lost any semblance of direction. On March 14, 1871, Barton County, Missouri, filed a lawsuit against him. Earp was in charge of collecting license fees that funded local Lamar, Missouri, schools, and he was accused of failing to turn in those fees.

On March 28, 1871, Earp and two others were charged with stealing two horses from a man in the Indian Territory, each animal valued at one hundred dollars. On March 31, James Cromwell filed a lawsuit against Earp, alleging that he had falsified court documents about the amount of money he had collected from Cromwell to satisfy a judgment.

On April 6, Earp was arrested for the theft, and bail was set at five hundred dollars. On May 15, an indictment against Earp and two others was issued. One of the men's wives claimed that Earp had gotten her husband drunk and then threatened his life if he wouldn't help him. Earp didn't wait for the trial. He climbed out through the roof of the jail and headed for Peoria, Illinois.

Wyatt Earp was legally an outlaw, having evaded charges in Lamar, Missouri. So what possessed him to do what he was charged with doing? Corruption, like today, was common in the governments of the West, sometimes even expected, to a certain degree. Anne Butler's *Daughters of Joy, Sisters of Misery* discusses the stance of the public on corruption within local law enforcement. She writes, "When they could not deny the corruption of city officials, they simply ignored it, convinced the judges, mayors, and police officials deserved anything they could get in return for the unsavory job of dealing with the criminal element."

If Earp did mishandle the funds, though it was of course illegal, it could still have been construed as socially acceptable. And being charged with horse theft? If he did it, he may have done it to escape an unjust charge of mishandling the county fund. But was horse theft justified? Earp was committed to his vision of justice, even if it did not always line up with the law.

Earp's biographer Stuart Lake reported that Earp took to hunting buffalo during the winter of 1871–1872, but Earp was arrested three times in the Peoria area during that period. Earp is listed in the 1872 city directory for Peoria as a resident in the house of Jane Haspel, who operated a brothel. In February 1872, Peoria police raided the place, arresting four women and three men: Wyatt Earp, Morgan Earp, and George Randall. Earp and the others were charged with "keeping and being found in a house of ill-fame." They were later fined twenty dollars plus costs for the criminal infraction. Earp was arrested for the same crime in May 1872 and again in late September 1872. It's unclear if he was a pimp, an enforcer, or a bouncer for the brothel.

Earp was arrested again on September 10, 1872, and this time he was aboard a floating brothel he owned named the Beardstown

Gunboat. A prostitute named Sally Heckell was arrested with him, and rumors claimed that she was his common-law wife.

His third arrest was described at length in the *Peoria Daily Transcript*, which referred to him as an "old offender" and nicknamed him the "Peoria Bummer," another name for loafer or vagrant.

Wyatt, aged four with mom, Virginia.
AUTHOR'S COLLECTION

DRAWN TO BOOMTOWNS

Wyatt Earp gravitated toward boomtowns where he kept a foot in each side of the law. Of course in those days there was no Social Security for "old age," no way to retire and live an easy life. Understandably, people did what they had to do to put food on the table. Sometimes it wasn't totally legal, but that didn't mean it was right. By 1874, he arrived in Wichita, Kansas, where a woman reputed to be his wife opened a brothel. Accounts are told that weapons were not allowed in town, but he needed to be able to protect his and his wife's interests. What better way to do that than to become a lawman in town so he could legally carry firearms? He worked as a deputy marshal for one year, and he developed a solid reputation as a lawman.

His stint as Wichita deputy came to a sudden end on April 2, 1876, when he took too active an interest in the city marshal's election. According to news accounts, former marshal Bill Smith accused Earp of using his office to help hire his brothers as lawmen. Earp got into a fistfight with Smith and beat him. Earp was arrested and subsequently fired for disturbing the peace, which ended a tour of duty that the newspapers called otherwise "unexceptionable."

When his brother James opened a brothel in Dodge City, Kansas, Earp joined him.

In the winter of 1878, he went to Texas to track down an outlaw, and he met John "Doc" Holliday, whom Earp credited with saving his life. Earp stated, "his quickness saved my life." In Dodge City, a man out to take down Wyatt Earp, aimed a gun at his back. Seeing the impending gunplay, Doc shouted, "Look out, Wyatt!" Before Earp could turn around, Doc drew his pistol and shot the man. Wyatt commented, "On such incidents as that are built the friendships of the frontier."

Continually drawn to boomtowns and opportunity, Earp left Dodge City in 1879 and moved to Tombstone, Arizona, with his brothers James and Virgil. The Earps bought an interest in the

Vizina mine and some water rights. They clashed with a loose federation of outlaw cowboys. Wyatt, Virgil, and their younger brother Morgan held various law enforcement positions that put them in conflict with Tom and Frank McLaury, and Ike and Billy Clanton, who threatened to kill the Earps.

The conflict escalated over the next year, culminating on October 26, 1881, in the Gunfight at the O.K. Corral, during which the Earps and Holliday killed three of the cowboys. In the next five months, Virgil was ambushed and maimed, and Morgan was assassinated.

THE VENDETTA RIDE—HE LIVED HIS LIFE ACCORDING TO A CODE THAT SEEMED RIGHT TO HIM

Without sufficient evidence to file charges in either case—Morgan's murder or Virgil's attempted murder—the suspected cowboys evaded justice. Thus began Wyatt Earp's Vendetta Ride. When justice had failed him, he and a posse sought to right the wrongs done to his family. This decision transformed Earp into an outlaw himself.

Earp, his brother James, and others murdered many of the Cochise County Cowboys. Curly Bill Brocius, Frank Stilwell, Indian Charlie, and Johnny Barnes were all killed within a two-week period. Earp and five others were indicted for murdering Frank Stilwell. Again, Wyatt Earp was on the wrong side of the law.

As a deputy US marshal, some of these actions were legally questionable. In fact, as Earp was hunting cowboys, Tombstone sheriff Johnny Behan had arranged his own posse, comprised mostly of cowboys and their supports, and was hunting Earp. Although some can argue the case that he was an outlaw at the time, Earp did not view himself that way. He felt he was executing justice and never doubted his actions.

Regarding the Vendetta Ride, the *Los Angeles Herald* wrote in 1882, "We know nothing of the inner history of this Earp

Vendetta, nor do we care a whit about how the quarrel started. . . .
The law should be supreme in Arizona as elsewhere. Every man
who is going about with arms in his hands, whether he belongs
to the Earps or the cowboys, should be made to lay them down."
Tucson's *Star* summarized the Democratic viewpoint: "One of the
worst features of the present state of outlawry which is being carried on . . . is that they are Deputy United States Marshals sworn
to protect and sustain the laws of the country. Instead, they have,
and are continuing to take the law into their own hands."

LAW ENFORCEMENT—IT'S A FAMILY AFFAIR
Wyatt Earp, who was deputy marshal in Tombstone, was not the
only Earp to serve on the side of the law. Brother Virgil, five years
older than Wyatt, was elected as one of two constables in Prescott,
Arizona Territory, in 1878. He was also appointed deputy US
marshal for Pima County and later Cochise County, Arizona.
Morgan, three years younger than Wyatt, served as a peace officer
in Butte, Montana, before becoming city marshal of Tombstone.
Warren, seven years younger than Wyatt, was a deputy city marshal in Tombstone (in 1900, Warren was shot and killed in a
Willcox, Arizona, saloon fight).

LIFE AFTER TOMBSTONE
A few years after the Vendetta Ride, Wyatt Earp's character
was again called into question. Wyatt, his brother Warren, and
two others were on the outskirts of Gunnison, Colorado, where
they reportedly pulled a gold brick scam by trying to sell a German visitor gold painted rocks for two thousand dollars. And it
was reported he'd done the same thing with "Mysterious Dave"
Mather in the tiny Texas Panhandle town of Mobeetie, originally
called Hidetown, in 1878.

Earp was a lifelong gambler and was always looking for a
quick way to make money. After leaving Tombstone, he went to
San Francisco, where he reunited with Josephine Marcus, and she

became his common-law wife. They joined a gold rush to Eagle City, Idaho, where they owned mining interests and a saloon. They left there to race horses and open a saloon during a real estate boom in San Diego, California. They moved briefly to Yuma, Arizona, before joining the Nome Gold Rush in Alaska in 1899. Earp and a partner paid $1,500 (about $47,000 in 2020 dollars) for a liquor license to open a two-story saloon called the Dexter and made an estimated $80,000 (over $2 million in 2020 dollars). While in Nome, Earp was arrested twice for minor offenses, including being drunk and disorderly.

The couple then left Alaska and opened another saloon in Tonopah, Nevada, the site of a new gold find. Around 1911, Earp began working several mining claims in Vidal, California, retiring with Josie to Los Angeles during the hot summer months.

THE BOXING MATCH HEARD ROUND THE WORLD

Like many men in the early twentieth century, Wyatt Earp enjoyed the sport of boxing, refereeing often. On December 2, 1911, Earp was a last-minute substitute referee in a boxing match between Bob Fitzsimmons and Tom Sharkey in San Francisco. Earp had already refereed over thirty matches. Fitzsimmons was favored to win, and he dominated the fight. Suddenly Sharkey dropped to the ground, clutched his groin, and rolled around on the canvas. Earp stopped the fight and awarded Sharkey the fight due to foul. The crowd replied with boos and hisses. Rumors flew that Earp had a goodly sum of money on Sharkey to win. The smear on his character from the fight stayed with Earp until the day he died.

Years later, Dr. Brookes Lee was accused of treating Sharkey to make it look like he was hit in the groin. In 1905, he told the *San Francisco Call*, "I fixed Sharkey up to look as if he had been fouled. I got $1000 for my part in the affair."

THAT'S A WRAP

The last surviving Earp brother and the last surviving participant of the Gunfight at the O.K. Corral, Wyatt Earp, died January 13, 1929. He was eighty. His pallbearers were prominent men: George W. Parsons, Charles Welch, Fred Dornberge, *Los Angeles Examiner* writer Jim Mitchell, Hollywood screenwriter Wilson Mizner, Earp's good friend John Clum from his days in Tombstone, and Western actors William S. Hart and Tom Mix.

Jim Mitchell wrote Earp's obituary. The newspapers reported that Tom Mix cried during his friend's service. Shocking her friends, Josephine didn't go to Earp's funeral, and it was reported that she was too paralyzed with grief to do anything after he died. Josie had Earp's body cremated and his ashes buried in the Marcus family plot at the Hills of Eternity, a Jewish cemetery (Josie was Jewish) in Colma, California. When she died in 1944, Josie's ashes were buried next to his. Their gravesite is the most visited resting place in the Jewish cemetery.

AFTERWORD

Although it was never incorporated as a town, the settlement formerly known as Drennan, located near the site of some of Earp's mining claims, was renamed Earp, California, in his honor when the post office was established there in 1930.

Wyatt Earp made friends with some early Western actors in Hollywood and tried to get his story told, but he was portrayed only briefly in one film produced during his lifetime: *Wild Bill Hickok* (1923). He even befriended and influenced early film stars of this genre, including Tom Mix, who served as a pallbearer at his funeral.

Despite the fact that he never drank, Wyatt Earp wasn't without his vices. He allegedly had a serious sweet tooth, particularly for ice cream. Luckily for him, there was a parlor that sold ice cream in Tombstone. He was said to have visited there nearly every day.

FINAL THOUGHTS—LAWMAN OR OUTLAW?

Yes, Wyatt Earp was both. As Trent Rosser wrote in *The Amarillo Pioneer: Rosser's Ramblings* on June 7, 2019, times were different then: "Today, he would be considered an outlaw. With all the things that he had allegedly done, from scamming to murder, he would not look favorably in the world today. Either way, Wyatt Earp was a bona fide lawman. We all make mistakes, and just because he was a great lawman, doesn't mean he was perfect."

There are at least three, maybe four, sides to every story, and now we know two—but will we ever know the real story? Probably not. Either way, Wyatt Earp will always be "the good guy in white."

BIBLIOGRAPHY

MILTON YARBERRY

Bryan, Howard. *Wildest of the Wild West*. Santa Fe, NM: Clear Light Publishers, 1988.

Bullis, Don. *New Mexico: A Biographical Dictionary, 1540–1980*. Vol. 2. Los Ranchos, NM: Rio Grande Books, 2008.

Bullis, Don. *New Mexico Historical Biographies*. Los Ranchos, NM: Rio Grande Books, 2011.

Bullis, Don. *Triple A Livestock Report*. Albuquerque, NM: New Mexico Cattlegrowers Association, 2014.

DeArment, Robert K. *Deadly Dozen: Twelve Forgotten Gunfighters of the Old West, Volume 1*. Norman, OK: University of Oklahoma Press, 2003.

Lowe, Sam. *Speaking Ill of the Dead: Jerks in New Mexico History*. Guilford, CT: Morris Book Publishing, 2012.

Metz, Leon C. *The Encyclopedia of Lawmen, Outlaws and Gunfighters*. New York: Facts on File, 2003.

Simmons, Marc. *Albuquerque: A Narrative History*. Albuquerque: University of New Mexico Press, 1982.

HENRY PLUMMER

Metz, Leon C. *The Encyclopedia of Lawmen, Outlaws and Gunfighters*. New York: Facts on File, 2003.

BURT ALVORD

Metz, Leon C. *The Encyclopedia of Lawmen, Outlaws and Gunfighters*. New York: Facts on File, 2003.

Wilson, R. Michael. *Legal Executions in the Western Territories, 1847–1911: Arizona, Colorado, Idaho, Kansas, Montana, Nebraska, Nevada, New Mexico, North Dakota, Oklahoma, Oregon, South Dakota, Utah, Washington and Wyoming*. Jefferson, NC: McFarland, 2010.

BILLY STILES

Eppinga, Jane. *Apache Junction and the Superstition Mountains*. Charleston, SC: Arcadia, 2006.

Find a Grave. "William Larkin Stiles (1871–1908)." www.findagrave.com.

Lowe, Sam. *Jerks in Arizona History*. Globe Pequot Press: Guilford, CT, 2012.

Metz, Leon C. *The Encyclopedia of Lawmen, Outlaws and Gunfighters*. New York: Facts on File, 2003.

O'Neal, Bill. *Encyclopedia of Western Gunfighters*. Norman: University of Oklahoma Press, 1991.

J. J. WEBB

Bryan, Howard. *Wildest of the Wild West*. Santa Fe, NM: Clear Light Publishers, 1988.

Bullis, Don. *New Mexico A Biographical Dictionary, 1540–1980*. Vol. 2. Los Ranchos, NM: Rio Grande Books, 2008.

Clavin, Tom. *Dodge City, Wyatt Earp, Bat Masterson, and the Wickedest Town in the American West*. New York: St. Martin's Press, 2017.

Lowe, Sam. *Speaking Ill of the Dead: Jerks in New Mexico History*. Guilford, CT: Morris Book Publishing, 2012.

Markley, Bill. *Wyatt Earp & Bat Masterson: Lawmen of the Legendary West*. Helena, MT: TwoDot, 2019.

Metz, Leon C. *The Encyclopedia of Lawmen, Outlaws and Gunfighters*. New York: Facts on File, 2003.

HOODOO BROWN

Bryan, Howard. *Wildest of the Wild West*. Santa Fe, NM: Clear Light Publishers, 1988.

Clavin, Tom. *Dodge City, Wyatt Earp, Bat Masterson, and the Wickedest Town in the American West*. New York: St. Martin's Press, 2017.

Garrett, Pat. *The Authentic Life of Billy the Kid*. Santa Fe: New Mexico Printing and Publishing Co., 1882. Reprinted in 1954; Norman, Oklahoma; University of Oklahoma Press.

Markley, Bill. *Wyatt Earp & Bat Masterson: Lawmen of the Legendary West*. Helena, MT: TwoDot, 2019.

Metz, Leon C. *The Encyclopedia of Lawmen, Outlaws and Gunfighters*. New York: Facts on File, 2003.

Weddle, Jerry. *Antrim Is My Stepfather's Name: The Boyhood of Billy the Kid*. Tucson: Arizona Historical Society, 1993.

"MYSTERIOUS DAVE" MATHER

Bryan, Howard. *Wildest of the Wild West*. Santa Fe, NM: Clear Light Publishers, 1988.

Clavin, Tom. *Dodge City: Wyatt Earp, Bat Masterson, and the Wickedest Town in the American West.* New York: St. Martin's Press, 2017.

Lowe, Sam. *Speaking Ill of the Dead: Jerks in New Mexico History.* Guilford, CT: Morris Book Publishing, 2012.

Markley, Bill. *Wyatt Earp & Bat Masterson: Lawmen of the Legendary West.* Helena, MT: TwoDot, 2019.

Metz, Leon C. *The Encyclopedia of Lawmen, Outlaws and Gunfighters.* New York: Facts on File, 2003.

DALTON BROTHERS

DeNevi, Don. *Western Train Robberies.* Millbrae, CA: Celestial Arts, 1976.

Metz, Leon C. *The Encyclopedia of Lawmen, Outlaws and Gunfighters.* New York: Facts on File, 2003.

Ward, Geoffrey C. *The West: An Illustrated History.* Boston: Little, Brown, 1996.

TOM HORN

Etulain, Richard, and Glenda Riley. *With Badges & Bullets: Lawmen & Outlaws in the Old West.* Golden, CO: Fulcrum Publishing, 1999.

Metz, Leon C. *The Encyclopedia of Lawmen, Outlaws and Gunfighters.* New York: Facts on File, 2003.

HENRY NEWTON BROWN

Burns, Walter Noble. *The Saga of Billy the Kid.* New York: Konecky & Konecky, 1953.

Lowe, Sam. *Speaking Ill of the Dead: Jerks in New Mexico History.* Guilford, CT: Morris Book Publishing, 2012.

Metz, Leon C. *The Encyclopedia of Lawmen, Outlaws and Gunfighters.* New York: Facts on File, 2003.

Utley, Robert M., *Billy the Kid: A Short and Violent Life.* Lincoln: University of Nebraska Press, 1989.

Wallis, Michael. *Billy the Kid: Endless Ride.* New York: W. W. Norton, 2007.

Weddle, Jerry. *Antrim Is My Stepfather's Name: The Boyhood of Billy the Kid.* Tucson: Arizona Historical Society, 1993.

ROBERT OLINGER

Brothers, Mary Hudson. *A Pecos Pioneer.* Albuquerque: University of New Mexico Press, 1943.

Bullis, Don. *New Mexico Historical Biography.* Los Ranchos, NM: Rio Grande Books, 2011.

Burns, Walter Noble. *The Saga of Billy the Kid.* New York: Konecky & Konecky, 1953.

Etulain, Richard, and Glenda Riley. *With Badges & Bullets: Lawmen & Outlaws in the Old West*. Golden, CO: Fulcrum Publishing, 1999.

Garrett, Pat. *The Authentic Life of Billy the Kid*. Santa Fe: New Mexico Printing and Publishing Co., 1882. Reprinted in 2018.

Lowe, Sam. *Speaking Ill of the Dead: Jerks in New Mexico History*. Guilford, CT: Morris Book Publishing, 2012.

Metz, Leon C. *The Encyclopedia of Lawmen, Outlaws and Gunfighters*. New York: Facts on File, 2003.

Rasch, Philip J. "The Olingers, Known Yet Forgotten." *Potomac Westerns Coral Dust 8*, February 1963.

Utley, Robert M. *Billy the Kid: A Short and Violent Life*. Lincoln: University of Nebraska Press, 1989.

Wallis, Michael. *Billy the Kid: Endless Ride*. New York: W. W. Norton, 2007.

ELFEGO BACA

Bryan, Howard. *Incredible Elfego Baca: Good Man, Bad Man of the Old West*. Santa Fe, NM: Clear Light Publishers, 1993.

Bullis, Don. *New Mexico: A Biographical Dictionary, 1540–1980*. Vol. 2. Los Ranchos, NM: Rio Grande Books, 2008.

Keleher, William A. *Memoirs: Episodes in New Mexico History, 1892–1969*. Santa Fe, NM: Sunstone Press, 2008.

Lowe, Sam. *Speaking Ill of the Dead: Jerks in New Mexico History*. Guilford, CT: Morris Book Publishing, 2012.

Melzer, Richard. *Legendary Locals of Albuquerque*. Charleston, SC: Legendary Locals, 2015.

Metz, Leon C. *The Encyclopedia of Lawmen, Outlaws and Gunfighters*. New York: Facts on File, 2003.

Simmons, Marc. *Albuquerque: A Narrative History*. Albuquerque: University of New Mexico Press, 1982.

JOHN HENRY SELMAN

Bullis, Don. *New Mexico: A Biographical Dictionary, 1540–1980*. Vol. 2. Los Ranchos, NM: Rio Grande Books, 2008.

Bullis, Don. *New Mexico Historical Biography*. Los Ranchos, NM: Rio Grande Books, 2011.

Clavin, Tom. *Dodge City, Wyatt Earp, Bat Masterson, and the Wickedest Town in the American West*. New York: St. Martin's Press, 2017.

Metz, Leon C. *The Encyclopedia of Lawmen, Outlaws and Gunfighters*. New York: Facts on File, 2003.

Metz, Leon C. *John Selman*. New York: Hastings House, 1966.

Nolan, Frederick. *The West of Billy the Kid*. Norman: University of Oklahoma Press, 1998.

Sonnichsen, C. L. *Pass of the North: Four Centuries on the Rio Grande.* El Paso: Texas Western Press, 1968.

Wallis, Michael. *Billy the Kid: Endless Ride.* New York: W. W. Norton, 2007.

WYATT EARP

Bryan, Howard. *Wildest of the Wild West.* Santa Fe, NM: Clear Light Publishers, 1988.

Butler, Anne. *Daughters of Joy, Sisters of Misery, Prostitutes in the American West, 1865–1890.* Urbana: University of Illinois Press, 1985.

Clavin, Tom. *Dodge City, Wyatt Earp, Bat Masterson, and the Wickedest Town in the American West.* New York: St. Martin's Press, 2017.

Climans, Kyle. *45 Gunslinging Facts about Wyatt Earp: The West's Most Famous Lawman.* Fascinate.com

Earp, Wyatt. *My Fight at the O.K. Corral.* Edited by H. P. Oswald. Scotts Valley, CA: Create Space Independent Publishing Platform, 2012.

Etulain, Richard, and Glenda Riley. *With Badges & Bullets: Lawmen & Outlaws in the Old West.* Golden, CO: Fulcrum Publishing, 1999.

Kirschner, Ann. *Lady at the O.K. Corral: The True Story of Josephine Marcus Earp.* New York: HarperCollins, 2013.

Lowe, Sam. *Speaking Ill of the Dead: Jerks in New Mexico History.* Guilford, CT: Morris Book Publishing, 2012.

Markley, Bill. *Wyatt Earp & Bat Masterson: Lawmen of the Legendary West.* Helena, MT: TwoDot, 2019.

Metz, Leon C. *The Encyclopedia of Lawmen, Outlaws and Gunfighters.* New York: Facts on File, 2003.

Monahan, Sherry. *Mrs. Earp.* Helena, MT: TwoDot, 2013.

Tefertiller, Casey. *Wyatt Earp: The Life behind the Legend.* New York: John Wiley & Sons, 1997.

ABOUT THE AUTHOR

New Mexico native Melody Groves loves Western history. Enchanted by the area where she grew up, as a youngster she and her family explored ghost towns, which sparked her imagination. Horses, tumbleweeds, the sky, and characters who impacted the Western mystique charged through her mind. They still do. Winner of numerous writing awards, she writes for *True West*, *Enchantment Magazine*, *New Mexico Magazine*, and *Wild West*, among others. In 2018, she won the prestigious National Press Women Award for her *True West Magazine* article on Albuquerque's first town marshal, who got himself (justifiably) hanged.